People Around the Wor

My biggest battles have not been persecution or intimidation, but fear, shame and condemnation. I have struggled for years trying to believe that God loved me personally. Mark's teaching is helping me understand that it is all about Him living in and through me. **–Pastor in Middle East**

You do not know me. I'm not anyone important. But none of that mattered to God. I received your book from my pastor and it changed my life.

– D. L. – Alaska

This revelation is growing and changing the way I see everything. I am all messed up, in such a good way, and I doubt that I will ever be the same! Thank you for pouring into our leaders. **– Steve Roberts –RevivalAsia**

I honestly do not know of anyone who has captured the true essence of the meaning of grace, as Mark Drake has. I want what he describes to be translated into my everyday, ordinary life. All of our international leaders are now using these materials. **–Micah Smith –Global Gateway Network**

Wow, wow, wow, thank you so much! We plan to use your materials to train as many people in South Africa as we can. Thank you for the amazing stuff you have produced. **– R. Borain – South Africa**

This is life-changing! How can we get more in Asia? **–Sandra –Singapore**

I highly recommend Mark's teaching to every believer who is worn out and wondering why things seem so difficult. **– Joe Morris – Mission/Africa**

Your teaching has finally gotten me to start relaxing and stop trying to earn so much. I'm not going to stop until it goes from my head to my heart.

–CeCe–Tennessee

I had just about given up...then I read your book and I have great hope once again! Thank you for helping change my life. **–D. H. –Michigan**

Thanks for messing up our lives! We are certain we will never be the same and we are extremely grateful to you. **–P. Feng –Malaysia**

Copyright ©2011 by Mark Drake
markdrake@aol.com
markdrake.org

Cover design by Henry Hoffarth, Creative Vision Design
creativevisiondesigncvd.com

Book layout by Joseph B. Geddes, Geddes Technology Consulting
joe@geddestech.com

Printing by Creative Vision Design
creativevisiondesigncvd.com

Printing for Asian edition by Samaron Enterprise
samaronprint@gmail.com

Back Cover Photo by Shalem Mathew
shalemphotography.com

ISBN: 978-0-9843433-1-7

All italics, bold print, underlining, and etc. are added by the author for emphasis and he takes responsibility for any inaccuracies in dates, places, events or biblical interpretations.

Scripture quotations are either author's paraphrase or taken from the NEW AMERICAN STANDARD BIBLE (NAS), Copyright 1960, 1962, 1963, 1968, 1971, 1972, 1973, 1975, 1977, 1995, The Lockman Foundation. Used by permission, www.Lockman.org, King James Version (KJV) or Holy Bible, New Living Translation, copyright 1996, used by permission of Tyndale House Publishers, Inc., Wheaton, Illinois 60189. All rights reserved.

All rights reserved. No part of this book may be reproduced or transmitted in any form or by any means, electronic, mechanical, including photocopying, recording, or by any information storage and retrieval system, without written permission from the author.

To my kids,

Lori, Aaron and Amanda,

who have watched me stumble along

on my journey and have, amazingly,

become my best friends.

I am a far better man because

you know me well and

still believe in me.

May you fully live in the freedom

this book attempts to explain.

Dad – June 30, 2011

God's Brilliant Cure
for Fear, Shame and Condemnation

1) Why Do I Still Feel So Bad?
2) But I Have A Good Reason To Feel Bad
3) Why Am I Still Paying A Price?
4) Maybe I Don't Believe What He Said
5) The Two Big Ones
6) How Does God Describe Himself?
7) These Directions Are Messed Up
8) What Did Noah Know That I Need To Know?
9) I Know How I Feel, But How Does God Feel?
10) Its My Parents' Fault
11) Draw Near Or Draw Back
12) The Problem With Fig Leaves
13) Is God's Presence A Reward For Holy Behavior?
14) Come Here And Be Changed
15) What Happens To Unholy People in God's Holy Presence
16) A Wee Little Man Gets God's Cure
17) Facing The Hard Truth About Myself
18) A Whole Lot Of Jacob In Me
19) Admit The Truth And Be Changed
20) God's Gift Of The Two Mirrors
21) What About Judgment And Wrath?
22) Why Was He Lifted Up?
23) Rainbows And Brainwashings
24) The Transforming Power Of Fellowshipping God
25) The Deliberate Choices: Feed, Focus And Faith

God's Brilliant Cure

For Fear, Shame and Condemnation

Mark Drake

Chapter One

Why Do I Still Feel So Bad?

Something was wrong. Something was clearly wrong with me...and with many of my most sincere friends. If the Christian life was supposed to be free of fear, shame and condemnation, why did I still feel so bad? Something had to be wrong.

As much as I hated to admit it, my understanding of New Testament Christianity had to be wrong because my life was just not working out right. After nearly thirty years of serving Christ, the battle in my mind and emotions had finally gotten so bad I became honest enough with myself, and with God, to ask some serious questions about what I was experiencing.

"Where is the peace that passes understanding?"

"Where is the 'joy unspeakable and full of glory'?"

"Where is the internal rest I am supposed to be living in?"

"Why do I feel such fear when things don't go right?"

> *"Why do I feel so ashamed when I fall short of perfect Christian living?"*
>
> *"Can I ever live up to that standard, anyway?"*
>
> *"Why do I battle so much condemnation when the Bible says I shouldn't have any?"*
>
> *"I know the Bible says He loves the whole world, but why do I worry that He doesn't actually **like** me?"*

I recently had an email conversation with a very sincere Christian couple who were struggling with the same tormenting fears I struggled with for years. They had read about my personal battles and the freedom I have now found in my journey with the Lord, and they wrote me about their own struggle.

> *"In your writings, you mentioned Christ living in and through us without guilt or condemnation. I have never known a Christian life without guilt or condemnation. I think I know what God's Word expects and I know that I fail miserably."*

I receive many letters similar to this because it seems to be the biggest battle most believers face; and people who have read my books know I can understand how they feel. Knowing what I now know about *What God is really like* and *How He really feels about me*, I wrote back to them.

> *"Living without fear, shame and condemnation is what the Lord wants for all of us, now, in this life. Those damaging beliefs come into our lives because of a faulty understanding of how God really feels about us and what He actually expects from us. I*

know this because I lived it and taught it sincerely for years, only to find out I was wrong. Sincere, but wrong."

Though I could completely understand how they felt, my heart broke for them when I received their response.

"I believe God expects perfection because that is what my conscience tells me and the Bible says 'be perfect as I am perfect'. When I do good, read my Bible, pray, etc., I feel like God is proud of me and I feel closer to Him when I try to make myself more holy.

*But, when I fall short, **which is all the time**, I feel like a complete failure and I just want to give up. I have given up a lot and I don't have much faith left. I pray that God has not cut me off.*

I can't imagine living the life you speak about. I hope I will live that life in heaven since I cannot find it here."

This sums up the battle I personally went through for years. And though I thought I knew the Bible well, I could not find answers for the questions that were destroying my faith.

The "*Expert*" Does Not Know What To Do

I had been in the "*ministry*" for over twenty-five years. I had traveled across the country and around the world preaching and teaching what I thought was the "*Good News*". I had been a pastor, helped plant churches, taught in bible schools and founded a ministry training center to prepare young preachers, teachers and missionaries to do the same.

Then I had my own personal, and very embarrassing, meltdown. Some people wiser than me have called it the "*dark night of the soul*". My "*dark night*" lasted for five years. That's one very long night. And all my "*expertise*" in biblical knowledge couldn't help me get out of it.

One dark night? I figured I could handle that. A week or a month, maybe. But five years was just way too much. And it left me helpless, hopeless and angry. Angry that God had the power to fix my internal mess, but apparently, He wouldn't. Angry that God had put too much on me after I was so sure He promised in His word that He would never give me more than I could handle; and I just couldn't handle this any longer.

But, most of all, I was angry with myself. Angry that after all these years of ministry and all these years of study, I just couldn't figure out how to get God to answer my prayers and fix this mess. Angry that no matter what I did, I couldn't muster up enough faith to get God to help me.

After five gut-wrenching years of watching everything I touched fall apart, I came to believe He wasn't keeping His Word to me. I knew that somehow it had to be my fault but I just couldn't handle all this internal failure any longer. I could no longer agree with King David when he said, "*I have never seen the righteous forsaken*". (Ps. 37:25)   I felt like I *was* being forsaken. I feared that I somehow deserved to be forsaken, but I couldn't figure out what He wanted me to do to change it. It became far more than I could handle.

For those interested in the gory details, I tell more of my personal story in my previous book, **God's Brilliant Plan** – *Searching for the Easy and Light Life Jesus Promised*.

I Am Going Fishing

So what does a *"minister"* do when he has given his entire life in service to God and now he no longer believes he can trust himself or his understanding of the God he has been serving? Well, he goes fishing.

That's what Peter did when his world came crashing down around him. When his disappointment with himself and with the One he had put his hope in ended in disaster, he went back to doing the only thing he felt he could trust in; fishing.

His retreat was to a boat and a net; mine was with waders and a fly rod. For the next year, instead of going to church, I went to the river. And I am eternally grateful that Jesus did for me what He did for Peter; He came and rescued me.

Jesus came to Peter while he was back out on the lake and showed him how he had mistakenly put his hope in a misunderstanding of the Father and a misunderstanding of the Father's methods and plans. I will be forever grateful that Jesus came to get me with a revelation of the same truths.

I had put my faith in a faulty view of what I believed *God was really like* and how *He really felt about me*. Something had to fundamentally change in the way I saw God. And, although I am still in the learning process, this book is designed to share part of my journey with you. My hope is that it will help you in your journey, too.

So What Do I Believe?

The great foundational bedrock of Christian theology is the answer to this question –

What legally happened to our sin at the cross?

Paul made the absolute declaration upon which all our faith ultimately hangs –

"He made Him who knew no sin to be sin on our behalf, so that we might become the righteousness of God in Him."

(2 Cor. 5:21)

There was a *legal* transaction made here and all true believers understand that salvation depends on what *legally* happened to the sin that separated us from God. In plain, practical terms, God took our sin (*past, present and future*), and placed it on Jesus when He was on the cross. He did this so that when Jesus died, our sin would *legally* die with Him. His death was the *legal* payment required of us; *"the soul that sins must die."* (Ezk. 18:20) He died in our place.

All that separated us from God, all which alienated us from the holy, just, righteous and infinitely perfect One, was placed on Jesus. God did this amazing act of love so that when Jesus died, the *legal* penalty would be paid in full and, *legally*, there would be nothing that could separate us from the Father.

Our sin died when He died.

When He died our sin died.

This is a ***legal*** issue and the law was ***legally*** satisfied. "*It is finished*" echoes down the ages as His pronouncement that all of our "*missing the mark*", all of our shortcomings, all of our "*falling shorts*" (*my youngest grandkids love that phrase*), all of our weaknesses were ***legally*** paid for; all the captives get to ***legally*** go free and "*whosoever will*" may come and ***legally*** get this free gift. This is ***legally*** right and true in every sense of the word…God's Word!

But Legal Satisfaction Doesn't "Feel" All That Great

Some of us preachers and teachers love to talk in legal terms, and certainly, some parts of the Bible speak in those terms. There are stacks of Bible verses to prove to us that all sin, which ***legally*** separated us from God, was ***legally*** satisfied at the cross.

"*The wages of sin is death.*" (Rom 6:23) That debt was ***legally*** paid for by death, and fortunately for us, it was paid for by the death of another. The *"other"* who took my sin was perfect in every way. He knew no sin. He was the spotless, perfect sacrifice that the law ***legally*** demanded.

Paul declares Jesus was the second Adam. Where the first Adam legally failed, the second Adam legally succeeded and all *legalities* were satisfied. And I am deeply, eternally grateful for this *legal* fact.

But there is something very *personally unsatisfying* about talking in only *legal* terms. It doesn't *feel* all that great. Something more than legalities have to be dealt with because our lives involve far more than abstract, impersonal laws. Our lives involve relationships; relationships with family, friends and, most importantly, relationship with the God who gave us life and calls us to Himself.

And I know that in my relationship with God, I am not living up to all the requirements I read about in the Bible. I know, after all He has done for me, there is still so much about me that is not like Christ.

Even though I know in my mind that the legalities have been settled, I have a nagging feeling deep inside about my personal, present failures. And, although my mind knows the Bible says He has to love me because of what Christ has done for me, I confess that I am worried about how He must actually *feel* about me. Does He actually *like* me?

Chapter Two

But I Have A Good Reason To Feel Bad

Let's say I do something wrong in my community. I break the law by reckless driving, I get caught, hauled into court and judged guilty...because I am. The story is in the newspaper and everyone who knows me knows what I did.

The policeman who caught me is angry with me because of my reckless behavior. The jury who found me guilty is angry with me because of my dangerous actions. And the judge who oversaw the process is angry with me because of my disregard for the law; and rightfully so.

With blatant, selfish disregard for the safety and well-being of others, I broke the law, disrespected civil authority and endangered the community. As a result of my selfish, dangerous actions, everyone is justified in being angry with me.

So there are at least three very real penalties I must deal with –

1. *The legal issue concerning the written law, which I violated as a lawbreaker.*

2. *How people feel about me as a lawbreaker.*

3. *How I feel about myself as a lawbreaker.*

And I can satisfy any one, or two, of these penalties, and yet, still *feel* miserable. And more than just an uncomfortable feeling, that miserable feeling can sabotage every area of my life.

Paying The Legal Price

Now let's suppose the judgment against me is financial and the punishment for my bad behavior is a huge monetary penalty. Let's suppose I don't have the money to pay the penalty. The only recourse I have if I don't pay the financial penalty is jail time. I do deserve it, I broke the law…but I can't pay.

Now, let's suppose, you step forward and pay the fine for me. You know I am guilty; they know I am guilty. But being my dear friend, you have mercy on me. You pull out your checkbook and pay the price I cannot pay; you pay my penalty.

The Law is satisfied. The judgment against me is paid in full. I am free from the *legal* penalty of my law-breaking. I am legally free from the penalty of the Law and no one can come at a later time and demand that I pay because the penalty has been paid in full. But I am still not free…*not really free.*

I am not free from the way other people *feel* about me as a lawbreaker and I am not yet free from how I *feel* about myself as a lawbreaker. Until those two issues are truly dealt with, I cannot be truly free.

Suffering The Relational Cost

The officer, the jury, the judge, the public; they are all still mad at me. At least, I think they are still mad at me. They know I am guilty and I am convinced they must still be angry with me for what I have done. And some of them may even feel that somehow I have gotten away with my crime because I didn't have to pay. Someone else paid the price and I get to go free.

And I do get to go free…from the penalty of the law. The law has been satisfied. The debt has been paid and I am *legally* free from that penalty.

But I am not yet free…*not truly free*. There is a price that still has to be paid. And it's a very personal, painful price.

I Think I Know What He's Thinking

I never had a reason to notice it before, but now I realize; I live just down the street from the judge. I drive by his house every day. And every day I think, *"I bet he's angry with me because he knows I am guilty, he knows I really did do the crime and he knows I didn't have to personally pay for it. He must believe I got away with something"*.

Then, for the first time, I realize his kids attend the same school my kids attend. I start noticing him at all the school functions and sporting events. And every time I see him I think I know what he's thinking..."*You're guilty and I am angry at you for what you did. And you didn't have to pay for it. Someone else paid the penalty so there is nothing I can do about it. But I am still mad because of your reckless behavior"*.

I can see it in his eyes, in the way he turns his head and looks away whenever I am around. At least, I think I can see it. I can just imagine what he must be saying to his wife whenever he thinks of me.

Even though I know the legal price has been paid, every time I see him it reminds me that I am guilty. I know I don't deserve to go free because I did do it and I didn't actually pay my own price; someone else did. I know I did the deed; I know I am guilty and I know I didn't pay. And every time I see the judge it reminds me that I *"did the crime but didn't do the time"*.

Even if that's not what he is thinking, I believe he is. And he is a constant reminder that there is still anger against me; the judge, the jury, the policeman…I am certain that they are all still angry with me and there is nothing I can do about it.

Then I Just Won't Care What People Think

One way to deal with this pain is to harden my heart to the point where I decide I just won't care what people think. And as Christians, there is a strong temptation to cover this thinking in clothes of self-righteousness and think it is actually godly. It can almost seem mature to say, *"I don't care what other people think about me. I am too mature to be bothered by what other people think."*

But there is great danger in this kind of thinking. It hardens our heart and that makes us arrogant, selfish and uncaring in our relationship to others.

The law of sowing and reaping is built into creation for some very good reasons. The reality is our actions affect everyone around us.

For example, adultery is forgiven at the cross but it's affect on the spouse and kids, and how they feel about what was done, is very real. And taking the attitude that *"I have been forgiven so I don't care what anyone else thinks"* actually reveals the very selfishness that caused me to indulge in my destructive, sinful behavior in the first place.

Love does care what other people think. Love does care what other people are feeling. Love does care about the pain our actions cause others. Love isn't manipulated or tormented by what other people think, but love does care what they are going through; especially if it's because of something we have done.

Paul tells us in 1 Cor. 13 what love does and doesn't do.

Love is patient and kind, never proud or rude. Love does not demand its own way. Love never gives up, never loses faith, never stops hoping. Love always prefers others' well-being above its own...and love empowers me to trust the Father to take care of me while I am deeply concerned about others.

But How Does The Real Judge Feel?

The only other option is to somehow deal with my fear about what others feel about me. But I can't really do that unless I deal with my fear of how I think God feels about me. He is the Real Judge and how He feels about me is most important because it governs how I feel about everything else.

And there is the problem. The Real Judge knows I am still not living up to the amazing price that was paid for me and He must be really mad about that, right?

Chapter Three

Why Am I Still Paying A Price?

If the legal debt has really been paid in full, why am I still paying a price? And I am paying a price. It's not money. It's not jail time. But it's eating away at me just the same. I *am* locked up because I'm a prisoner in my own mind and emotions.

No matter how much my friend paid to cancel my legal debt, no matter how sorry I am for what I did, I am still tormented by what I imagine to be the justified anger of the judge. The judge may not actually be angry with me, but I *imagine he is*. And as long as I am convinced he is angry, it eats away at me, because I know no matter what I do, I can't change how he feels. And that is the real price; and it's a painful, personal, tormenting price.

The Real Judge Must Still Be Angry, Right?

I know Jesus paid the *legal* price for my sin. I know He took my place and satisfied the law. And I know the Real Judge had to let me go free. And even though I suspect He might not really want to, He has to let me go free because Jesus paid it all.

But somehow that doesn't make me *feel* all that much better because I also know I am not holy enough for Him, yet. So the Real Judge must still be angry with me, right?

After all, I am constantly reminded that my daily life still doesn't reflect the perfectness of Jesus. I know I still fall short in so many ways. And it's only amplified when I go to a church service and participate in communion.

For years I was taught, and I taught others, that before you take the bread and the cup, you better get everything right between you and the Lord. And I have to be honest, just thinking that the *legal* penalty has been paid doesn't remove the guilty conscience I battle when I think of my daily life.

I find myself still tormented with thoughts like David thought, *"My sin is ever before me"*. (Ps. 51:3) I know I am not yet living up to the sacrifice Jesus made. And that scares me.

A Freudian Slip?

Something revealing just happened. When I first wrote that last paragraph I misspelled the word *"scares"* and wrote the word *"scars"*. Then, when I read it again, I realized that this kind of fearful thinking about how the Real Judge must feel about me does *scare* me...but it *"scars"* me, too.

It wounds me, it steals my confidence with God and I don't know what to do about it. When I live only in the ***legal*** reality of the cross, it may solve my eternal problem, but it doesn't solve the daily life problem of why I still worry about God's anger towards me.

John addressed this confidence-stealing problem when he wrote, *"Beloved, if our heart does not condemn us, we have confidence before God".* (1 John 3:21) And this confidence issue is what troubles me.

Legally, I know the Real Judge has to let me go free. My problem is – *I suspect He might not really want to.* He *has* to...because Jesus paid it all.

And this is what condemns my heart because *legalities* don't solve my heart problem. I worry about how God really *feels* about me. And this fear twists the way I read His Word.

What We Say Compared To What He Said

I have heard all the passionate, well-intended sermons. In the interest of full disclosure, I have preached most of these things, myself.

"Jesus gave His all, how can you do anything less?"

"Look at Him on the cross, see His suffering for you... now live a life that's worthy of that suffering!"

"Unless you take up your cross, as He took up His, you are not worthy of Him."

"The holy God cannot look upon your unholy life, so when He looks at you, He doesn't see you, He only sees Jesus."

*"If He is not Lord **of all**, then He can't be your Lord **at all**!"*

That last statement is from a song we sang forty years ago in the early days of the Jesus Movement. The repeating line said, *"If He's not lord of everything, then He's not lord at all"*. I know the author was deeply sincere and passionately in love with the Lord and I don't fault him at all. I have written songs that caused similar, unintended, consequences. I don't sing them anymore.

These kinds of statements, no matter how logical they sound or how well intended they are meant to be, still produce feelings within us that the Bible boldly declares have no place in the life of a New Covenant believer. And far from being just *"motivational exhortations"*, statements like these, whether spoken or sung, reinforce destructive beliefs that steal our confidence, fill us with insecurity and leave us with a terribly wrong view of God and how He really *feels* about us.

Though the Bible declares to us, *"There is now no condemnation to those who are in Christ"* (Rom. 8:1), these kinds of ideas fill us with condemnation and shame.

Though the Bible reassures us, *"There is no fear in love"* (1 John 4:18), these kinds of ideas fill us with fear of the very One who is perfect love; the One who deeply desires to heal and empower us.

Though the Bible promises us, *"Do not worry about what you will eat or drink because you are highly valued by the Father"* (Luke 12:24 paraphrased), these kinds of ideas lead us to believe that unless we are doing God's *"perfect will"* in every way He may not take care of us.

It is becoming painfully obvious to me that there is a big difference between what I say and what He says. I am finding that there is a big difference between what I say *He said* and what He *actually said.*

Maybe I Don't Know What He Actually Said

In my own journey in the Lord, I am finding that most of my struggles come from either –

> **(1)** *Not knowing what He has said about Himself and His feelings toward me*, or

> **(2)** *Taking partial verses out of context and twisting them to mean something completely opposite of what He intended.*

Frankly, I am embarrassed at how often I have done *(and continue to do)* this.

Throughout this book, I will attempt to share with you things I once deeply believed only to find that I had built a very shaky life on a very faulty foundation. And though I have spent all my adult life trying to be a *"scholar"* in the written word, I want to reassure you, you don't have to be an expert to have a life free of fear, shame and condemnation.

You don't have to know Hebrew or Greek. You don't have to have a theological degree *(it may be best that you don't)* and you don't have to lock yourself away in a monastery so you can devote yourself to an isolated life of study. The early gentile believers didn't do any of this. They didn't have any of the study helps we have. They didn't benefit from any of the technology we have. Most of the early gentile believers didn't have the Old Testament. They didn't even have the New Testament!

And yet, they matured in their faith, grew in their trust of the Father, planted enduring churches throughout the known world and shook the Roman Empire to its core. Not by rebellion or political power, but by lovingly extending a heavenly Kingdom that was based on a very different view of the Almighty God than what I have had over the years. And, though I desperately wanted to believe what they believed, being a *"scholar"* of the Word didn't help me.

Asking The Hard Questions

Throughout the Book of Acts we see how Paul was constantly contending with Jews who refused to read the Old Testament just as it was written. They violently rejected Paul's message about the Messiah because they already had their beliefs about what the Word of God said and they were not going to let the simple truth get in their way.

But when Paul came to a town named Berea, he found a different group of people. These Jews were willing to ask the hard questions about what they believed. As they listened to this foreigner tell them that they might be seeing God's Word incorrectly, Acts 17:11-12 tells us *"...they received the word with great eagerness, examining the Scriptures daily to see whether these things were so. Therefore many of them believed..."*

Verse 10 says they were *"more noble-minded"* because they were eager to ask themselves hard questions about what they believed and then compare that to what the Word actually said. They weren't interested in the *latest revelation or the newest thing.* They wanted to know the *original revelation, the oldest truth.* They wanted to know what God actually said and what He meant when He said it. I haven't always been like them but I want to be.

We don't have to be experts but we must be willing to ask the hard questions about what we believe. We have to be willing to have our beliefs challenged and trust the Spirit of truth to guide us into all that is actually true about God and about ourselves. (John 14:17, 15:26, 16:13)

And we must come to trust that our Father will guide us by His Spirit and give us wisdom and revelation in the written Word. What God truly *says in our hearts* will always agree with what He has *already said* in His Word. And when it doesn't, it's not God talking to us. It's a different voice!

The Pharisees were experts in the Old Testament. They spent their lives studying the same Bible Jesus read. And yet, they completely misrepresented the nature and heart of God to the people and completely missed the central message of the scripture they thought they knew so well.

> *"You search the Scriptures because you think that in them you have eternal life; it is these that testify about Me..."*
>
> (John 5:39)

Jesus was the central theme of everything they read, yet they missed the whole thing. And when I get honest enough to truly look at my lack of "*heart confidence*", I have to wonder about myself, *"What have I missed?"*

Chapter Four

Maybe I Don't Believe What He Said

In my previous book, <u>God's Brilliant Plan – *Searching for the Easy and Light Life Jesus Promised*</u>, I shared how deeply Matt. 11:28-30 bothered me. This is where Jesus tells the sincere, searching Jews that the life He wants for them, and any who will believe in Him, will produce rest and relationship instead of exhausting labor and tormenting religion.

His promise is that being yoked together with Him will result in a life that is actually ***easy*** and ***light***. To my embarrassment, I had to admit that I didn't actually believe what He said.

Matt 11:28-30 – *"Come to Me, all who are weary and heavy-laden, and I will give you rest. Take My yoke upon you, and learn from Me, for I am gentle and humble in heart; and you shall find rest for your souls. For My yoke is easy, and My load is light."*

After years of trying to *"live the Christian life"*, I just didn't believe this kind of *easy* and *light* life was ever what God intended. It just sounded too simple, too...*easy*. I just could not believe that was what Jesus actually meant.

But for those who have read **God's Brilliant Plan**, you know that my personal discovery was that God's eternal plan has never been for us to try hard to *"live the Christian life"*.

My life-changing discovery was that God's intention has always been to teach us how to cooperate with Jesus as the Holy Spirit works to live His life ***in*** and ***through*** us. And I am continuing to learn that these two ways of living, *working hard to live the Christian life and ethic* or *letting Him live His life in and through me,* are diametrically opposed to each other. These two ways of living are as opposite from each other as day is from night, as black is from white, or...as law is from grace.

I have had people from all over the world respond to **God's Brilliant Plan** by telling me of the great freedom, peace and joy they now have. Their response has been deeply rewarding to me. But I have also had responses from people who reacted to the title and its perceived meaning, by telling me that there is no such thing as a Christian life that should or could be *easy* and *light*.

They have pointed out that the Christian life is supposed to be hard, demanding, narrow and difficult to find. Some have vigorously told me that I was misleading my readers to think that this life should somehow be easy and light, when, in fact, we are commanded to take up our cross and die daily. How can that be *easy* and *light*, they ask?

This Is Not Working
The Way It's Supposed To Work

My response to these sincere brothers and sisters in Christ has always been the same; I understand the dilemma, I really do. I sincerely lived in that painful struggle for years. I passionately preached and taught the *hard and narrow way* around the world.

But, in all honesty, I had to admit my life was not working the way Jesus said it should. I did not live in unwavering peace and abounding joy as the early believers did. My peace and joy were directly dependent on how well my circumstances were going at any given moment.

He said, *"You shall find rest for you souls"*. But my ability to live in rest came from having everything work out the way I thought it should. He said, *"Do not worry about what you will eat or drink"*. But my ability to be free from worry was tied to how quickly my prayers were answered and if they were answered in the way I thought they should be.

And when things didn't happen *when* I thought they should, or *where* I thought they should or *how* I thought they should, my peace was eaten up by worry and anxiety. And then the tormenting questions would come flooding in –

"What did I do wrong?"

"And whatever it is, am I being judged for it?"

"Why didn't I read my Bible more?"

"Why didn't I pray more?"

"Why didn't I get the word out so more people could pray with me?"

"Why didn't I get it out on more email prayer lists, on Facebook, mySpace, or maybe eHarmony?"

"Am I too proud?"

"Am I being judged for my pride?"

*"Was I just asking for the will of God when I should have been asking the **perfect** will of God?"*

"And how will I know the difference, anyway?"

Each of these questions has a seed of truth, a half-truth, in them. But so did the challenges the devil made to Jesus when He was tempted in the desert. Everything the devil said was taken out of Old Testament scripture. But Jesus knew the heart and intention of the One who gave those scriptures. He knew *What God is really like* and *How He really feel about us*.

It seemed to me that each time I began to ask if I have truly done enough for God to really love and bless me the way I want Him to, the next question was always, *"How much is enough?"* In my confusion and fear, I knew enough about the Bible to know my life was not working the way it was supposed to work.

Changing The Way We See God

I found that I could not possibly believe what Jesus promised in Matt. 11:28-30 unless I radically changed the way

I looked at God. Clearly, I did not see the Father the way Jesus saw the Father. I had developed a way of seeing God that was based entirely on the *legal* aspect of the cross. My view was void of the *relational* message given through the cross.

My problem started coming clear to me. I didn't really believe what God has said about Himself; *What He is really like* and *How He really feels about me.* And though admitting my unbelief was a very hard truth to face about myself, it has put me on the greatest, most rewarding search of my life. And, although I have come a long way in this search, this remains the on-going battle.

Could my lack of understanding about *What God is really like* and How *He really feels about me* be the root cause of all these tormenting questions?

> *Why do I still battle with such feelings of condemnation when there is supposed to be no condemnation?*
>
> *If He freely paid my penalty, why do I feel He is still so angry with me when I fail?*
>
> *Why do I so frequently feel He must be ashamed of me?*
>
> *Why do I so rarely feel truly loved and fully accepted?*
>
> *Why do I still wonder what I did wrong every time something bad happens?*

Why are my feelings of peace and joy so dependent on how well things are going at any given moment?

Why can't I enjoy my progress without immediately feeling guilty about where I am still missing the mark?

And why do I feel so afraid that my lack of Christ-likeness may cause God to not help me the next time I'm in trouble?

Chapter Five

The Two Big Ones

After well over forty years of international ministry, I now find myself joyfully reduced to a place of extreme simplicity in my relationship with God. I believe my life, my peace, my joy, my ability to find the will of God, and my power to endure adverse circumstances comes directly from how I answer these two simple questions –

1 – What is God really like?

2 – How does He really feel about me?

By saying the answers to these two eternally important questions are *simple,* I am not implying the answers are elementary to the point of meaningless nor that they won't require a battle for us to keep believing them. On the contrary, these are the two most important questions you will ever answer…and you will have to fight to keep answering them in every season of your life.

By saying the answers to these questions are *simple*, I am not implying the answers are easy to arrive at or easy to hang on to. In fact, the battle for the hearts and minds of the human race is decided by the way each person answers these two questions. And the battle to get these answers rooted deep within our hearts and minds will continue throughout our natural life.

Every time trouble comes, every time things go bad, every time we experience an outcome that doesn't seem to line up with what we thought would be *"good"*, our hearts are challenged by how we answer these two questions. And though we are told in His word that we must keep battling in this life (*fight the good fight of faith* 1 Tim. 6:12), we can be assured about our eternal end.

One day, when we see Him, this battle will be settled forever because we will then *"know as we are known"* (1 Cor.13:12) and all these questions will be eternally answered within us!

Asking The Right Questions

Forgive me if these two questions sound too simple or too elementary to be included in a discussion about the Almighty God. I can get much more theological than this. I've read the books, I've taken the courses, and I've been to the conferences. Actually, I taught many of them for years.

I know we can talk in much more lofty, technical and esoteric terms. We can ask about the divine, eternal character of God or the transcendent nature of God. We can do an in-depth study on the many names of God, the Hebraic view of God, the Grecian view of God and so on, and so on…

But those are not the questions we really want answered. And if we got them answered I'm not sure it would make any real difference in our lives. In fact, after working hard to get those answers, it didn't make any real difference in my life, at all. It didn't seem to work for the Pharisees, either.

We have to ask the right questions if we want to get the right answers. And it seems to me that these are some of the things most of us really want to know –

> *"What are You really like, Father?"*
>
> *"And since You are THE Father, how will that work in my life?"*
>
> *"How are you going to treat me when things go wrong?"*
>
> *"What should I expect You to do when trouble comes?"*
>
> *"What will Your reaction be when I mess up?"*
>
> *"I am asking because I'm pretty sure I'm going to mess up…with some regularity."*

And if the measurement for our human lives is the perfect nature of Christ, then messing up and falling short is to be expected and shouldn't come as a surprise to Him…or to us.

No Illusions Of Perfectness Here

Certainly the early writers knew this –

> *"For all have sinned and come short of the glory of God"*
>
> (Rom. 3:23)

> *"If we say that we have no sin, we are deceiving ourselves and the truth is not in us"*
>
> (1 John 1:8)

> *"For we all stumble in many ways"*
>
> (James 3:2)

> *"Not that I have already obtained it or have already become perfect, but I press on so that I may lay hold of that for which also I was laid hold of by Christ Jesus. Brethren, I do not regard myself as having laid hold of it yet..."*
>
> (Phil 3:12-13)

These New Testament writers had no illusions that they were anywhere near the perfect image of Christ. They were not displaying some kind of phony humility or somehow trying to condescend and *"relate to the laity"*.

They were stating a fact which they were willing to regularly admit; in this life we fall short of the glory of Christ's perfect nature. They seem to have clearly understood that this life is an on-going journey in God and there is no perfect destination in this life.

Our Eternal Destination

Don't misunderstand me. They fully believed there was a perfect destination. But they knew it would come when we finally stand before His unfiltered presence and are forever changed by His glory to be like His Son. They were absolutely convinced that they would one day be made like Him.

John said it like this –

"We know that, when He appears, we shall be like Him..."

(1 John 3:2)

Paul declared this way –

"For if we have become united with Him in the likeness of His death, certainly we shall be also in the likeness of His resurrection..."

(Rom. 6:5)

And again –

"...for the trumpet will sound, and the dead will be raised imperishable, and we shall be changed."

(1 Cor. 15:52)

These men were completely convinced that, though we are *"in process"* now, we are predestined to be **made** into the image of His Son forever!

> *"For whom He foreknew, He also predestined to become **conformed to the image of His Son**, that He might be the first-born among many brethren..."*
>
> (Rom 8:29)

They were so convinced of their eternal place with the Father, they had no fear of being honest about their shortcomings, now, in this life. They were so convinced that this life is one of continually being changed by the Spirit that they did not live with insecurity in their relationship to the Father, now, in this life.

Clearly, these men were answering the *two big questions* in a way that gave them tremendous confidence with God; a confidence that was not based on how perfectly they were doing everything but on what they believed about God – *What is He really like* and *How does He really feel about us*.

It seems clear from what these early believers wrote, they believed the normal New Testament Christian life was frequently three steps forward and two steps back...or as I sometimes experience; two steps forward and two and a half back! By the way, people like Peter seemed to experience life like that, too, so we are in good company.

So, the two big questions, *"What is God really like"* and *"How does He really feel about me",* have become absolutely essential questions for me to ask, keep asking...and get answered!

Here Comes the Judge

All relationships, human or divine, begin with an understanding of what the parties involved are really like. The ability to relate to one another is based on some basic understanding of each other's personality, nature, values and character. If a person is mean, angry, critical and judgmental, you will relate very differently to them than you would to someone who is kind, gentle, thoughtful and loving.

If God is first, and foremost, the righteous Judge of the earth, then everything He does toward us will begin with judgment. Our relationship with Him will be based on the comparison of His holiness and our lack of it; His righteousness and our lack of it; His perfectness and our lack of it.

If this is *what God is really like,* then our relationship with Him will always be one where He is judging our behavior compared to His, weighing us in the balance and, because we are human and He is not, He will always *"find us wanting"*. We will be constantly falling short and He will be constantly passing judgment upon us.

But is this true? Is this view of God biblical? Is this the way the early believers related to God? Is this view of God the one they declared to be the "*Good News*"?

As I have traveled around the world, it seems clear to me that most people, most believers, do indeed view God as, first and foremost, the Righteously Angry Judge. And we seem to think He really likes to pour out judgment.

Now that we have satellite TV available virtually everywhere in the world, just listen to the religious commentators –

Hurricane in New Orleans...Judgment.

Tsunami in Asia...Judgment.

Earthquake in California...Judgment.

Drought, famine in a Muslim country...Judgment.

Aids epidemic...Judgment.

You voted for who?...Here comes judgment.

Then I listen to my own self-talk.

My wife gets really sick...*what did I do wrong or what did she do wrong?*

One of my kids makes bad choices...*I didn't pray enough or maybe I didn't confess the word enough.*

I don't get the promotion I prayed for...*I guess I didn't "sow" enough to that TV evangelist.*

Righteous behavior, more prayer, sacrificial giving; these are all good, important and beneficial things. But this kind of thought process reveals that I actually believe I have to earn the Father's blessing and care. These kinds of thoughts and beliefs about the nature of God will result in either faith or fear, worry or confidence, peace or turmoil.

This will inevitably happen because, without consciously realizing it, I have decided *What God is really like* and *How*

He really feels about me based on my misguided understanding. I have made a judgment about the nature and heart of God.

But, what if I am wrong about Him?

Chapter Six

How Does God Describe Himself?

We can find volumes of human descriptions of what God is assumed to be like. There are great books written about the names of God, the attributes of God and the nature of God. And I suppose they all bring something of value to the discussion. But how does God describe himself?

Moses had a front row seat when God choose to give the definitive description of *What He is really like* and He described Himself by telling us *How He really feels about us*.

This self-description took place in Ex. 33-34. One very important aspect of this story is that it came in response to the repeated rebellion of the people.

Moses had gotten so angry because of the unfaithfulness of Israel, their forsaking of the true God and building an idol to lead them back to Egypt, he broke the stone tablets with the Ten Commandments...which God had cut out with His own finger. Talk about destroying some valuable memorabilia, actually signed by THE author!!!

After the outright rebellion of the people as they prostituted themselves to other gods and Moses' angry response, God calls him back up on the mountain. My guess is he went in much fear and trembling. If there was ever a time for the Judge to come forth and flex His *"mighty right arm of power"*, this was it.

But instead of the expected fire and brimstone...

Here's what happened –

Moses tells God how confused he is about himself, the people, the plan and the apparent failure so far. He really is confused about this whole deal and he's blaming a good part of it on God. Moses, the one who complained in the beginning of this adventure that he shouldn't be chosen for this task because he couldn't speak, now speaks. Boy, does he speak!

> *"You said You really liked me but then You sent these people with me and they're a bunch of rebels. You said You were taking us to the Promised land but this group of rebels You gave me is never going to make it. And I'm starting to get the feeling You are thinking about wiping them all out and starting over but I don't see how that's going to work. And by the way, I didn't want to come back here anyway and I don't like these people and I am really starting to regret going to check out that 'burning bush' deal. You really pulled me in with that one."*
>
> *(OK, if you actually read the story in Ex. 33 it's not exactly like that, but it's pretty close.)*

Then, partly out of anger and partly out of desperation, Moses pleads with God –

"Moses said, 'I pray You, show me Your glory!' And He said, 'I Myself will make all My goodness pass before you..."

(Ex. 33:18-19)

Moses cries out to see God's glory, which is typically viewed as His awesome power, His terrifying strength, His righteous vengeance or the consuming fire of His judgment. It certainly seems as if Moses is asking God to come in His mighty power, fry the people and fix this mess.

How does the *"Judge"* respond?

*"I will make all my **goodness** pass before your eyes."*

Wow, that caught me off guard. I don't know what Moses was expecting God to do but that's not what I was expecting. His people had betrayed Him. After all He did to rescue them from slavery in Egypt; all the signs, all the wonders, all the mighty works, they quickly build an idol and start back into Egypt. What ingrates!

How does the *"Judge"* respond?

*"I will make all my **goodness** pass before your eyes. You need to see just how good I am. You don't know Me as I really am. You have been slaves all your lives, all your parents' lives, all your grandparents' lives...for over 400 years. In your minds, you have just traded one tyrant, Pharaoh, for another, Me.*

*That's because you don't really know me. Let me show you **what I am really like** and **how I really feel about you.**"*

Apparently, God knew the cure for the failure of the people would be a revelation of *What He is really like* and *How He really feels about them*. God places Moses back into the far end of a cave in the side of the mountain so his frail, mortal body will be protected from God's unveiled presence. And God passes by.

I love this story. Moses doesn't actually see God because no mortal can actually see God and live. We would just fry; we would evaporate. So Moses sees *"where God just was"*.

As one translation says Moses saw God's *"hindquarters"*. Moses saw God's *"behind"*. (*You can see why my grandkids love it when I tell this story*) What Moses saw was so supernatural that it temporarily altered the molecular structure of the exposed skin on his face and he radiated light for many days afterwards.

When Moses finally comes back down the mountain he has to wear a bag over his head because the light that shone out of his skin was too much for the people to look at!

As God passes by where Moses is hidden, He begins to describe Himself:

"Then the LORD passed by in front of him and proclaimed, "The LORD, the LORD God, compassionate and gracious, slow to anger, and abounding in lovingkindness and

truth; who keeps lovingkindness for thousands, who forgives iniquity, transgression and sin..."

Listen To God's Own Description Of Himself:

Compassionate...

Gracious...

Slow to anger...

Abounding in lovingkindness...

Abounding in truth...

Keeping lovingkindness for thousands...

Forgiving iniquity...

Forgiving transgression...

Forgiving sin...

This is where God *begins*! Of all the things God could say to describe Himself (*and He's infinite, so there's a whole lot to say*), He begins with compassion, love and forgiveness. This was God's response to an obstinate, rebellious people who were forsaking Him; and to His chosen man who just said, *"I don't see how You are going to pull off this 'chosen people, promised land' thing"*.

God's response was to declare how good He is!

And He is not just generally good to the universe, or the angels, or the "great beyond" somewhere, but He is specifically good *to the people*...full of compassion *for the people*...slow to anger *toward the people*...always forgiving *of the people*!

God wanted Moses to understand. God knew Moses had to understand that all His goodness, compassion and forgiveness was not theoretic, poetic or esoteric; it is all *for the people*, the rebellious people, the obstinate people, the failing people. This is *"what God is really like"*... for the people who need it the most!

So Their Sin Doesn't Matter?

It's about here that something within me is tempted to think, *"Wait a minute, are you saying that God is so loving, so compassionate and so forgiving that sin doesn't matter?"*

And then I am amazed at myself! I am amazed that I would so quickly move from God's awesome description of Himself and jump to a conclusion that would demand judgment and punishment, first. When God begins by telling me how much He loves me and how His goodness is the ***cure*** for my badness, why do I want to rush ahead to judgment, assuming the worst about Him and His feelings toward me?

Why would I want to start where He ends? He starts by declaring how good He is but I want to begin with the judgment and punishment part. Why would I do that so quickly and easily?

Could it be because of the misguided way I see Him? Could it be that I don't really believe He is the way He describes Himself? And does that way of thinking cause me to misunderstand adverse circumstances in my life? And even if I am reaping from what I have sown, does that automatically mean it's God's anger...could it be His love?

When all the New Testament writers talk about trials and tribulations as something to rejoice in...*and I think they have lost their minds*...could that be because they saw God very differently than I do? Could it be that they really believed in the way God described Himself?

The End of the Garden Party

As we will see in a later chapter, this tormenting and self-destructive tendency to assume the worst about God began with our parents in the Garden. They quickly swallowed the lie that God, who had been nothing but loving toward them, would now be angry and reject them because they failed.

They now believed that the God who had cared for their every need would now condemn them and that the Almighty who had used His power to only help them would now be the One they better hide from. It seems they were so willing to believe this lie.

Amazing...and heartbreaking...because I find this same mentality working so powerfully in me.

So, is God so good that our sin doesn't matter? Of course, sin does matter. It mattered in the garden. It mattered for

Israel in the wilderness; and it matters for me today. Sin is demeaning, decaying, deceptive, and destructive. It hardens our hearts and darkens our minds. And though it is a real problem for us, it is not a *"problem"* for God because He has the cure.

If you read on ahead in our Exodus 34 passage you will see that God does address His response to those who are determined to cover their sin and not confess it. After telling us how good He is and how He wants to forgive any and all who ask, He then says –

"...yet He will by no means leave the guilty unpunished..."

(Ex. 34:7)

The message should be crystal clear. The *"guilty"* are those who have refused to accept God for **what He is really like** and **how He really feels about us**. If we refuse the cure then we have chosen the disease. That is not God's choice, it's ours. That is not God's desire, it's ours.

After saying how much He loves us and how He really wants to forgive iniquities, transgressions and sins, He then says, *"But if you choose to refuse the free gift of forgiveness I offer, you are choosing to face the consequences of rejecting My free gift of forgiveness."*

God is, in fact, *completely loving* **and** *completely just*. His love doesn't conflict with His justice, nor does His justice conflict with His love. Instead, His love and justice completely compliment and fulfill each other. *Mercy and* *justice are married in Him.* I can't wrap my tiny mind around how those two things could perfectly exist in complete harmony in my life…which is why He is God and I am not!

The key is in seeing that the only way I can rightly understand God's justice is to begin by understanding His amazing love.

The Angry God of the Old Testament

I know how it feels to struggle with what seems to be a vengeful, angry God in the Old Testament but a loving, gentle Jesus in the New Testament. This has been a theological and practical dilemma for ages. And my struggle should tell me how much I have misunderstood about *what God is really like* and *how He really feels about me.*

The loving, gentle Jesus of the New Testament is the same one who says, with both love and justice, *"There is no other way to the Father but through Me".* (John 14:6) This is the same compassionate Jesus who says, *"…he who does not believe has been judged already, because he has not believed in the name of the only begotten Son of God."* (John 3:18-19)

Most Christians don't read this and think Jesus is being mean, vengeful or demanding. We understand, because of His love for us, that He is telling us there is only one way that life can truly work. And because He loves us, He has made a way for us to have that abundant life. It's easier for us to see that Jesus is both fully loving and fully just.

But this is the same God who says in the Old Testament, *"I am full of mercy, compassion and forgiveness, and because of My love for you, I want you to know this is the only way life will work. If you reject my free gift then there is no other remedy for the results you have chosen"*.

If we look back at Ex. 34 and start reading (*and believing*) at the wrong place, we would think God is, first of all, an angry Judge, full of vengeance, looking for those He can punish. But God starts with His compassion and love for us! And if we start where God starts, we then see Him as He really is; a loving Father who is full of compassion, abounding in love and mercy, ready to help all who call on Him.

It really does matter if you *start at the right starting place*. Of course, this is exactly what our adversary does not want us to do.

And thus, the deception begins.

Chapter Seven

These Directions Are Messed Up

I travel…a lot. After an average of one hundred different planes and just about that many different beds each year, the mystique of travel tends to wear off.

Don't get me wrong, I absolutely love what I do, the places I get to go and the people I meet…well, most of them, anyway. And I can't even imagine what the early apostles would have given to be able to travel as we do today.

That is part of the problem with whatever age you live in; it's hard to imagine what earlier times were like and it's hard to be grateful for what you have. It's just easier to complain and take things for granted.

Travel may not always be fun but it's frequently exciting.

I've been in Boston's Logan International Airport when a storm knocked out the power and every flight was immediately canceled, leaving tens of thousands of frightened travelers stranded…in the dark…for two days.

I have helped the National Guard set up row after row of green folding cots so travelers could get a little sleep when snowstorms shut down Chicago's O'Hare Airport. I have flown with small, foreign airlines where we couldn't land until the livestock was cleared off the landing strip.

I have sat on a lonely runway in a tiny plane while part time employees jump-started the engine with the battery of an old, battered pick-up truck. And then heard the pilot say in broken English, as we started down the tiny runway, *"We'll be OK as long as I don't kill it!"*

And I have flown in bush planes taking off and landing nearly anywhere possible – on water with pontoons, on snow with skis and on gravel bars with balloon tires. It does tend to keep you praying.

Where am I?

After flying on several planes and crossing several times zones, I have awakened in a dark room more than once and wondered, *"Where am I?"* That's when I reach for the light I hope is there and look for anything familiar to jog my memory.

"Where am I?" is a frequent thought I have when getting into a rental car in a strange city. But modern technology has come to my rescue. Granted, my grandchildren understand this technology much better than I do, but I have learned enough of the basics to make it work for me.

These Directions Are Messed Up

Two basic navigation tools in the old days were the sun and moss growing on the side of trees. But for modern travel we have computer programs like MapQuest, Goggle Maps and portable GPS units. With the computer programs, I enter the location I am leaving from and the destination I want to arrive at; and it prints out turn-by-turn directions. So I take my printed directions, get in the rental car and begin to read –

1. Go two blocks and turn right.

2. Go 1.2 miles and turn left.

3. Go one block to the first entrance ramp and enter freeway heading south.

4. Go 8.5 miles and take exit to stop light.

5. Turn right at light and go two blocks to final destination on right.

I follow these simple, clear directions and arrive safely at my destination. Or I get lost as a goose and start yelling at the directions and those stupid computers.

Here's how that scenario happens:

I plan to leave from the hotel and drive to the location where I will be speaking. You know how it works; the *"Man of God"* has come from far away to bring the latest revelation. *(You know, the same "man of God" who is now yelling at the stupid computer!)*

I have overslept, and as I rush to get ready, I cut my finger. I have no Band-Aids in my travel bag, and not wanting to drip blood while I minister, I drive to the nearest drug store. Having administered first aid to my injured finger, I pull out of the drugstore parking lot and start following my directions.

1. Go two blocks and turn right.

2. Go 1.2 miles and turn left.

3. Go one block to the first entrance ramp and enter freeway heading south.

4. Go 8.5 miles and take exit to stop light.

5. Turn right at light and go two blocks to final destination on right.

Wait a minute, I am at number 3 on the list of directions and there is no entrance ramp and no freeway heading south. I know I did exactly what the directions say but I can't find the freeway anywhere.

I get on my cell phone and dial the only number I have for the meeting location. Someone answers, I tell her my problem and she sweetly asks, *"Where are you, sir?"*

I don't know where I am…because I am lost. I followed the directions exactly and now I am lost. I am running out of time and she wants me to tell her where I am. Of course, if I knew where I was I wouldn't be lost. I don't actually say this out loud because I am the "*man of God*", but I am thinking it pretty loudly.

I am running out of time and options, so I begin to pray, asking the Holy Spirit to lead me. I know He knows where I am; He knows everything. But apparently He's not speaking to me right now. Or perhaps I can't hear Him over the sound of my yelling.

So I start looking for signs; street signs, spiritual signs, a heavenly glow in the right direction, or if one of my hands would just heat up so I would know which way to turn...

Of course, you know my problem (*other than my bad attitude, I mean*).

I didn't start from the right place. There's nothing wrong with the directions. They are exactly right. But they show me leaving from the hotel. I left from the drugstore. If I start from the wrong starting place, the right directions will lead me to the wrong destination. There's nothing wrong with the directions, I just didn't begin at the right starting place.

Let me say that again...

If I start from the wrong starting place, the right directions will lead me to the wrong destination.

Reproved, Rebuked And Corrected by GPS

Now we have these miracle gadgets called "GPS" units. I have no idea how they work, my grandkids can explain it, but I can't. I just plug it in, type in where I want to go, and a lovely voice tells me step by step, turn by turn what to do. And if I make a wrong turn, she corrects me, recalculates and guides me onward. Admittedly, she does sound a bit perturbed with me when she says *"Recalculating!"*

It's like having my very own rebuker in the car with me. But I am learning to receive computerized correction with some measure of humility. Besides, I sound stupid talking back to a computerized voice…although that doesn't stop me from doing it occasionally.

The beauty of a GPS unit is that it begins by telling me where I am. Even when I am lost it knows right where I am. It even puts a blinking dot right on the map to say, *"I know you don't where you are but I do. You are right here. Now turn around and go the other way!"*

The GPS of the Word

This is what I am supposed to let the Word of God do for me. It will tell me where to begin. When I fail, the Word wants to bring me back to the correct starting point. When troubles come, it wants to return me to the right starting place. The Word will tell me where God starts and where He wants me to start. It will point out the correct beginning place for me if I will just read it *as it is written*.

But tradition has messed me up. I have heard so much teaching that starts at the wrong place and takes me to the wrong conclusion, I think it's right. And then I repeat that to others when I teach and they start at the wrong place and the directions lead them to the wrong conclusion. We think we are doing it right…but it's not producing the peace and joy it is supposed to produce. So we just try harder to make it fit with what we've been told. And round and round we go.

"Recalculate"

We don't it on purpose. We don't even know we are doing it. That's the problem with deception. When I am deceived, I don't know it. If I knew it, I wouldn't be deceived. But I know something is wrong because where the Bible says there is no condemnation, I have condemnation. Where the Bible says I should have unwavering peace and abounding joy, I seem to have recurring worry and nagging fear. And I keep hearing this faint voice saying, *"Recalculate. Get back to the right starting point".*

How many times do we begin by thinking God is first, and foremost, the holy, righteous Judge, and then feeling overwhelmed by a sense of judgment. But in our Ex. 34 passage, we see God telling us He sees Himself, first of all, as the great lover of all mankind. He declares Himself to be full of compassion for all mankind, abounding in mercy for all mankind, always willing to forgive all mankind.

Last of all, if we refuse the cure of His love and compassion, then justice demands that we reap the consequences. But that's not His choice or desire. He wants broken people like us to begin at the right starting place so we can enjoy His cure for our brokenness.

God comes to me talking about His *cure* for me. But my fearful heart tends to hear only of His judgment toward me.

Jesus did the same thing when He came. He came talking about the cure but the Pharisees wanted to debate judgment. Jesus came talking about how much the Father loved the people but the Pharisees wanted to talk about how God should punish the wrongdoers.

The Pharisees studied the same scriptures Jesus studied but they came up with a completely different picture of God. Jesus started at one place; they started at another. Apparently, Jesus started in Ex. 34 seeing the Father as loving, compassionate and forgiving. The Pharisees read Ex. 34 and started with *"...yet the guilty will not go unpunished!"*

John 3 tells us where Jesus began with His answer to *"What is God really like"* and *"How does He really feel about me"*.

Who Knows the Father Best?

Jesus, the Son, knew the Father better than anyone. John said He was sent from the *"bosom of the Father"*. (John 1:18) Jesus said He came to show us the Father and *"if you've seen me, you've seen the Father"*. (John 6:46, 14:9) Who better to describe the Father than the Son?

So when speaking to Nicodemus, an expert in the Law and, supposedly, an expert in the revelation of God in the Old Covenant, Jesus uses this as His GPS starting point –

> *"For God so loved the world that he gave his only Son, so that everyone who believes in him will not perish but have eternal life. God did not send his Son*

into the world to condemn it, but to save it. There is no judgment awaiting those who trust him. But those who do not trust him have already been judged for not believing in the only Son of God."

(John 3:16-18 NLT)

So where does Jesus begin? *"God loves the world so much…I was not sent to condemn!"* This is His starting point. His divine GPS is set to always, always, *always* begin here.

He's going to get to judgment at the end of this statement but it is only for those who refuse to begin at His starting point. In fact, He goes so far as to say, *"There is no judgment awaiting those who trust him".*

Wait a minute.

I feel judged every time I fall short. I feel condemnation every time I miss the mark of Christ's perfection. In fact, the very meaning of Paul's word, **condemnation**, is *"a fearful expectation of judgment or punishment".* And I have felt that fearful expectation with great regularity.

If there is no condemnation to those who are in Christ Jesus and if there is no judgment waiting for me right around the next *"circumstantial corner"*, then why do I feel this way?

Chapter Eight

What Did Noah Know That I Need To Know?

Imagine you are sitting in your church service one Sunday morning and the special guest speaker begins like this–

"I have been diligently studying the Bible and I have come to share the important revelation I have seen.

God is a holy God. He is the most holy God and He cannot tolerate unholiness. Yet the world is growing more and more unholy; America is becoming more and more unholy and God cannot abide it. It grieves His heart and offends His righteousness. So God is left with no other recourse but to come in judgment.

And I have come to tell you that God is going to again cleanse the earth as He did with Noah. God is angry and He is again going to flood the earth and wipe out unrighteous humanity. God has sent me today to tell you we must prepare for another flood."

What would you think? What would you say? What Bible passage would you look for to either verify or disprove what the speaker has declared to be true?

Simple Sunday School Truth

My guess is that even young Sunday school students would dispute the *"truth"* of this declaration by simply saying, *"What you are saying cannot be true since the rainbow is God's promise that He will never flood the earth again"*. Most of us would know enough about the Bible to say that whatever God is going to do concerning judgment, it won't be with a flood since He made what He called an *"everlasting covenant"* that He will never flood the earth again.

Gen. 9:8-17 tells the story of God promising, *"Never again will I destroy all flesh with the flood"*. It is here that we are told of the rainbow that would be the reminder of this eternal covenant so Noah's descendants wouldn't go crazy every time it rained. Based on this promise, this *"everlasting promise"*, we would point out that the Bible teaches us what this speaker is saying just can't be true…and hopefully this speaker would not be invited back.

Of Course, God is Mad...Isn't He?

Now, what if someone came and taught that God cannot possibly be mad at us? What if they taught that even with all the seemingly clear Old Testament evidence of God's anger, wrath and punishing judgment, something has changed, something is different now? What if they boldly proclaimed God has sworn He would never be angry at us again?

What would we say? Where would we look in our Bibles to prove that this isn't just another watered down, liberal, *"sin doesn't matter"* heresy?

But what if this doubtful, possibly heretical declaration was actually true? What if God did promise He will never be angry at us again? What difference would it make? How would we think differently about Him? How would we approach Him differently? Or would we just ignore Him since we wouldn't need to fear His anger anymore?

Or, is it possible, that some people, perhaps a lot of people, might run to Him for the help they have needed for a long time but were afraid He wouldn't give because they were sure He was mad at them?

But if He is mad about our sin, if He's angry because we have failed so miserably, I'm not sure we should try to get too close to Him. It could be dangerous. After all, He is jealous, isn't He? He is vengeful, isn't He? He is angry at us for our gross lack of holiness…isn't He?

What Legally Happened To Sin On The Cross?

Isaiah 53 is the great Messianic chapter that tells us in the most profound, prophetic detail about the coming of Christ, His rejection and crucifixion. This chapter contains the most amazing foretelling of the cross and exactly what would happen there.

This is where we are told that God put the sins of the whole world upon Him and the legal debt was paid. When Paul wrote in 2 Cor. 5:21, *"He made Him who knew no sin to be sin on our behalf…"* he was referring directly to the legal truth we find in Isaiah 53.

> *"Surely he took up our infirmities and carried our sorrows, yet we considered him stricken by God, smitten by him, and afflicted. But he was pierced for our transgressions, he was crushed for our iniquities; the punishment that brought us peace was upon him, and by his wounds we are healed. We all, like sheep, have gone astray, each of us has turned to his own way;* **and the LORD has laid on him the iniquity of us all.**"

(Isa. 53:4-6 NIV)

This is the great legal declaration that the penalty was paid at the cross. The debt was settled at the cross. All that was owed because of our sin has been paid in full at the cross. The debt of law has been eternally, legally satisfied…at the cross.

But something else happened at the cross and it's of extreme importance to my daily life, my mental health and my emotional well-being. The next chapter, Isaiah 54, tells all about it. And yet it took me thirty years to read it and understand it.

And it has an amazing reference to Noah, the flood and the power of the promises God makes to us if we will believe.

And here it is –

> *"For this is like the days of Noah to Me, when I swore that the waters of Noah would not flood the earth again; **so I have sworn that I will not be angry with you nor will I rebuke you.** For the mountains may be removed and the hills may shake, but **My lovingkindness will not be removed from you**, and **My covenant of peace will not be shaken**, says the LORD who has compassion on you."*
>
> (Isaiah 54:9-10)

God Is So Serious About This, He Swears

This is one of the most dogmatic, declarative statements in the whole Bible; and I didn't even know it was there for thirty years. Oh, I had read it many times but I never really *saw* it. And I never connected it to the truth in the preceding chapter of Isaiah 53.

No true theologian believes chapter 53 is just for the Jews at some future time. Virtually all Christians believe Isaiah 53 is for anyone, at anytime, who puts their faith in Jesus Christ. He was wounded for us, He was bruised for us, He was crushed for us, and the sins of us all were placed upon Him. All of salvation hangs on this truth.

If all the promises in Isaiah 53 are true for anyone who will believe that *"the Lord has laid on Him the iniquity of us all"*, then the promises in Isaiah 54 are true for anyone who will believe the same God made these promises, also.

Listen to the extreme, emphatic language God uses in making the promises of chapter 54–

"This is like the days of Noah to Me..."

"I swore to Noah..."

"I now swear to you..."

"Until the mountains are removed..."

"Until the hills shake..."

These are definite, absolute statements. God is swearing something here that He declares will stand forever...for any who will believe the promises of chapter 53. And what is God swearing to?

"I will not be angry with you!"

I know we may not be able to even begin to understand or explain what this might mean in our everyday lives, but we must return to this right starting place...*God has* **sworn** *He will never be angry with anyone who believes Isaiah 53.*

Could This Be True?

Lest we think God is talking about something else, or somebody else, let's look at the larger context.

"For a brief moment I forsook you,

But with great compassion I will gather you.

In an **outburst of anger**

I hid My face from you for a moment,

But with everlasting lovingkindness I will have compassion on you, Says the LORD your Redeemer.

For this is like the days of Noah to Me,

When I swore that the waters of Noah

Would not flood the earth again;

So I have sworn that I will not be angry with you

Nor will I rebuke you.

For the mountains may be removed

And the hills may shake,

But My lovingkindness will not be removed from you,

And My covenant of peace will not be shaken,

Says the LORD who has compassion on you."

(Isaiah 54:7-10)

Read the whole chapter. As direct result of the sin-offering of the Messiah in chapter 53, chapter 54 makes a whole list of amazing promises.

"Shout for joy...fear not...don't be ashamed...don't feel humiliated...My everlasting lovingkindness...my compassion...I will never be angry...I will not rebuke...I will lay your foundations...I will build you...no weapon formed against you shall prosper...I will vindicate you!"

These are amazing, incredible promises that run through the entire chapter of Isaiah 54. If these things are true for any who believe the offering made in chapter 53, why are we still battling with fear, shame and condemnation about our lack of perfectness?

Could it be that we have believed the legal aspect of what happened to our sin on the cross but we've missed the other half of what was accomplished?

Could it be that we have believed the eternal aspect of salvation but we have missed the part that most directly affects our everyday walk with God?

Could it be that we have missed fully half of the real reason for the cross?

I know I missed it for almost thirty years of my Christian life…and it nearly killed my faith.

Chapter Nine

I Know How I Feel, But How Does God Feel?

Jesus was the full and complete legal offering for sin...once and for all! Every type and shadow of sacrifice and offering in the Old Testament that was legally required was fulfilled in Him. He is the *substance* that fulfills every *shadow* of the Old Testament. He who knew no sin was made to be sin for us so that when He died, the legal penalty for sin was paid...once and for all...for any who would believe.

> *"When you were dead in your transgressions...He made you alive...having forgiven us...having canceled out the certificate of debt consisting of decrees against us...He has taken it out of the way,* **having nailed it to the cross.***"*
>
> (Col. 2:13-14)

The legal *"certificate of debt against us"* was satisfied when the Father placed it all upon Jesus and *"nailed it to the cross"*.

As wonderful as this **legal** knowledge is, there remains something very unsatisfying about knowing only this part of what was done on the cross. Paul fully understood this dilemma when he wrote about the struggle of *"sin-conscience"*.

Something Still Doesn't Feel Right

The word *"conscience"* is used several times in the New Testament and it means the *"inner awareness or belief that something is morally wrong"*. God put that awareness within people. We are hardwired with it. It's meant to be an inner *"moral compass"* to help keep some measure of order within a fallen world. Whether a society has a biblical foundation or not, there are certain behaviors that people know are just not right. Even when there is not a written law, some things just don't *feel right*.

Paul speaks of this when he says the Gentiles, who did not have the Law of Moses, still had an *"inner witness"* because *"...their conscience bearing witness and their thoughts alternately accusing or else defending them..."* (Rom. 2:15).

The problem with conscience is that our adversary can use it against us. Because conscience is internal and subjective, we can be deceived. Our conscience cannot always be trusted. My adversary, the devil, can use my conscience to *"alternately accuse or defend me"*. This is why he is called the accuser of the believer. (Rev.12:10) And if we don't read the scripture as it is plainly written, it becomes easy to mistake the accuser's voice for the voice of the Holy Spirit.

This is the problem with looking at the cross and only seeing the legal debt having been paid. It leaves me convinced the Judge is angry with me because now that I know better, I should be doing better. I still feel ashamed because I know the reality of my unholiness is still there and the Holy God must be offended at me. He must be ashamed at my inability to live like His Son. He must embarrassed to call me His child when I am still so unlike Christ. But is all this actually true?

Why Do I Feel Like This?

God understands this human dilemma of how we *feel*. This is why He wants us to understand that something more is accomplished through the cross. And the *"something more"* has to do with how we *feel* about Him and how we should *feel* about ourselves.

Speaking of the limitations of the legal payment in the Old Covenant, Hebrews 9:9 says, *"...accordingly both gifts and sacrifices are offered which cannot make the worshiper perfect in conscience."*

Part of the dilemma with the Old Covenant was it couldn't do anything about the people's consciousness of failure, their awareness of sin. But as long as they were more aware of their failings then they were aware of God's goodness, it dramatically affected their ability to relate to God, to know

Him, to draw near to Him and be changed by Him. It deeply affected how they felt and how they thought God felt about them.

It is this consciousness, this *self-awareness*, which keeps making us start at the wrong starting place...and arriving at a fearful destination. God starts with His love and compassion; we tend to start with His anger and judgment. Jesus started with how much the Father loves the world but the Pharisees started with how the world needs to be judged and punished. Not them, of course, but the "*other people*".

Start Where Jesus Started

Please, don't misunderstand me. It has taken me years to arrive at this perspective without feeling that I was betraying what the Bible says about eternal judgment. Jesus certainly talked about eternal judgment and hell, although it now seems clear to me that He did so with grief and sadness; and He never started there. He regularly started with how the Father *felt* about the people.

> "*For God so loved the world...There is no judgment awaiting those who trust him.*"
>
> (John 3:16-18 NLT)

> "*Fear not, little flock, it is the Father's good pleasure to give you the kingdom.*"
>
> (Luke 12:32 KJV)

Allow me to speak very untheologically.

(That may not be a real word but it should be.)

The yearly sacrifices under the Old Covenant still left the people *feeling bad*. *(I know that's poor grammar but I'm trying to make an important point.)* They knew the legal debt was paid but they still felt ashamed about their inability to live godly. They were still embarrassed by their lack of perfect God-likeness. They were still convinced God was mad at them for their weakness.

As a result, their *"fear of God"* was an unhealthy, tormenting fear that caused them to draw back from God instead of drawing near to Him. *(Remember this draw near/draw back issue...it becomes really important latter on!)*

Heb 10:1-4 tells us that part of the problem with the Old Covenant sacrifices was that they constantly reminded God's people of how much they failed rather than washing away their awareness of sin so they could freely draw near to God. When they were focused on their failure they couldn't focus on God's goodness and draw near to Him for His eternal *cure*.

> *"The old system in the law of Moses was only a **shadow** of the things to come, not the **reality** of the good things Christ has done for us. The sacrifices under the old system were repeated again and again, year after year, but they were never able to provide **perfect cleansing** for those who came to worship. If they could have provided perfect cleansing, the sacrifices would have stopped, for the worshipers would have been purified once for all time, and their **feelings of guilt would have disappeared**. But just*

the opposite happened. Those yearly sacrifices reminded them of their sins year after year. For it is not possible for the blood of bulls and goats to take away sins."

(Heb. 10:1-4 NLT)

Listen to the problem again.

"If the (Old Way) could have provided perfect cleansing... their feelings of guilt would have disappeared. ***But just the opposite happened.*** *Those yearly sacrifices reminded them of their sins year after year."*

The shadow of the Old Way kept making the people feel more self-aware, not God-aware. But we must remember, Jesus is the *substance* that fulfills all the *shadows* of the Old Way. The shadow of the Old Way can never do what the substance of the New Way can do. Even though obedience to God's commandments concerning sacrifice in the Old Way provided forgiveness, it could never wash their conscience. It could not wash away their feelings of unholiness and it constantly made them self-aware instead of God-aware.

Hebrews 9:9 tells us the Old Covenant sacrifices could deal with the legal issue temporarily, but it could never free our conscience from fear, shame and condemnation. But listen to the writer's declaration of what the cross does-

"For if the blood of goats and bulls...sanctify for the cleansing of the flesh, how much more will the blood

*of Christ...**cleanse your conscience**...?"* (Heb. 9:13-14)

The act of the cross provides the legal remedy that forever purchases our salvation. But the work of His Spirit provides the practical, personal remedy that cleanses my conscience, washes my awareness and changes how I feel about myself; because it changes how I believe God feels about me. He did all this, not just for legalities, but because He loves me!

When I see the cross is not just a legal act, but the ultimate act of God's love for me, my conscience (*my heart*) is convinced God is no longer mad at me. Then I want to draw near to Him for His cure, rather than draw back in fear.

"...since we have a great priest...let us draw near...in full assurance of faith, having our hearts sprinkled clean from an evil conscience..."

(Heb. 10:21-22)

Wow! *"... let us draw near...in full assurance of faith, having our hearts sprinkled clean..."*

He wants us to draw near to Him with full assurance having our hearts cleansed from an evil awareness about ourselves...and a fearful awareness about Him. He is not mad at us. He put His anger on the cross.

What *Two* Things Happened At The Cross?

Every true believer believes that God put our sins upon Jesus on the cross. We believe that when Jesus died, our sins died with Him. But something else happened on the cross. And the importance of this second aspect of the cross is huge!

God not only put the eternal reality of the sins of the whole world on Jesus, He also put His justified anger about those sins upon Jesus. Everything God justly felt about the world's rebellion, everything He felt about the offensive choices mankind has made; He placed it all on Jesus. He did this so that when Jesus died, not only would the eternal consequence of sin die, but how God *felt* about our sin died with Him.

Let me say that again....

How God felt about our sin died with Jesus.

If I were sitting in a coffee shop with you right now talking about this amazing truth, I would put my hand on your arm and say, *"Repeat this after me, 'How God felt about my sin died when Jesus died. God's justified anger died when Jesus died!'."*

Think about it. No, I mean, really ***think*** about it. Through the cross, not only did the eternal consequence of our sin die, but how God *felt* about our sin died, too.

All of God's righteous, well-deserved anger at the sin and rebellion of all mankind was placed on Jesus. Past, present and future. All of the righteous indignation, all of the justified wrath, all the offense to His holiness; it was all placed on His Son.

Everything a perfectly holy God would *feel* about sin and rebellion was placed on Jesus...everything God ***felt***! And

Isaiah 53:10 declares that it pleased the Father to do this so there would be many *"offspring"*…that's us!

And all He asks us to do is to believe Him. And in believing, He will do His life-changing work inside of us.

How The Righteous God Felt

In the previous chapters we looked at how we so often feel about our failures, our sins, and our weaknesses. But this promise is about how the righteous, holy, infinitely perfect God *felt* and what He did with those feelings. And when we come to believe this truth, it radically changes how we feel about ourselves...and about Him!

Jesus was hung naked before the whole world so our shame would be placed on Him. He was stripped bare so all of the humiliation for our moral failure would be placed on Him. He was turned over to His tormentors and *"smitten of God"* so all of our embarrassment from missing the mark so badly would be placed on Him.

All this was done so that when He died, God's anger would die with Him. The horror of the crucifixion was done so that when He died, God's wrath would die with Him. He was bruised, wounded and smitten so that when He died, God's holy, righteous judgment would die with Him. It was all done so that when He died, the way God *felt* about our sin would die with Him.

Why does this matter? Why is this so important?

So that nothing would keep us, the ones He so deeply loves, from running to Him, seeking Him, drawing near to Him and truly coming to know Him!

So why, when I fall short, do I draw back from Him instead of drawing near to Him?

Perhaps it's my parents' fault.

Chapter Ten

It's My Parents' Fault

If we are going to truly understand *What God is really like* and *How He really feels about me*, we must begin with the very first time human beings messed up. The answers to our two big questions come clear when we see how God reacts to the very first act of willful disobedience; the very first act of *"I know better than You do, God"*.

This is the question my heart desperately wants answered-

"How does God feel about people who really mess up?"

And more personally-

"How is the Holy God going to react when I act in my own unholiness and mess up?"

All we have to do to find the answer to this all-important question is…begin at the beginning. We have to start where God starts. And we have to be willing to read just as it is written. Not the way we have come to interpret it over the years, but just the simple way in which it is given to us. And remember, this tells us about God, His nature and His heart.

In The Beginning or The Big Inning

Genesis 3 tells us the story of the *"fall"*, the beginning. Or as a friend of mine likes to call it, *the Big Inning,* because the outcome of the whole *"game"* hangs on understanding what actually happened in the garden.

This story has been told and retold throughout the known world for thousands of years. Adam, Eve and the *"apple"* has become a metaphor for countless moral lessons...and mocking jokes. And we believers know this story very well. At least, we think we do.

But when we read it just the way it is written, we may find a truth that is radically different from what we have mistakenly come to believe. The truth of this original sin, and God's reaction to it, has everything to do with *What God is really like* and *How He really feels about us.*

(I know there is a strong temptation to skip over bible passages we think we already know so we can get to what the book's author says next. ***Please don't****. I have highlighted certain words to call our attention to critical points we will discuss in greater detail later.)*

Gen. 3:1-14

1 Now the serpent was more crafty than any beast of the field which the LORD God had made. And he said to the woman, "Indeed, has God said, 'You shall not eat from any tree of the garden'?"

2 The woman said to the serpent, "From the fruit of the trees of the garden we may eat;

3 but from the fruit of the tree which is in the middle of the garden, God has said, 'You shall not eat from it or touch it, or you will die.'"

4 The serpent said to the woman, "You surely will not die!

*5 "For God knows that in the day you eat from it **your eyes will be opened**, and **you will be like God**, knowing good and evil."*

*6 When the woman saw that the tree was good for food, and that it was a delight to the eyes, and that the tree was desirable **to make one wise**, she took from its fruit and ate; and she gave also to her husband with her, and he ate.*

*7 Then the **eyes of both of them were opened**, and they knew that they were naked; and they sewed fig leaves together and **made themselves** loin **coverings**.*

*8 They heard the sound of the LORD God walking in the garden in the cool of the day, and the man and his wife **hid themselves from the presence** of the LORD God among the trees of the garden.*

*9 Then the LORD God **called to the man**, and said to him, **"Where are you?"***

*10 He said, "I heard the sound of You in the garden, and **I was afraid** because I was naked; **so I hid** myself."*

*11 And He said, "**Who told you that** you were naked? Have you eaten from the tree of which I commanded you not to eat?"*

*12 The man said, "The woman **whom You gave** to be with me, she gave me from the tree, and I ate."*

13 Then the LORD God said to the woman, "What is this you have done?" And the woman said, "The serpent deceived me, and I ate."

What Do We Know? What Don't We Know?

We can only go on the information we are given. There is much about this story the Holy Spirit doesn't tell us.

We don't know how much time passed from when they were created to when the fall actually happened. Apparently it was long enough for them to get to know their Creator and understand their job in the garden.

We don't know what kind of relationship they previously had with the "*serpent*". We must be careful here to understand the use of metaphor in scripture.

Talking serpent, dragon, roaring lion, god of this world: these are all metaphors used to describe an evil spiritual being which you and I cannot fully comprehend in our natural world. The devil, our adversary, is not actually any of these things. However, these word pictures help us understand what he is "*like*". Don't carry the metaphors beyond what the text says.

We don't know how God appeared to Adam and Eve when He came into the garden. God is spirit, and yet, He apparently came into the garden each afternoon (*in the cool of day*) to walk and talk with His creation in a way they could see Him, hear Him and communicate with Him.

This appears to be the regular routine. After they worked all day in the garden, cultivating and keeping it (Gen.2:15), God came into the garden to fellowship with them.

Wow, I would give a lot for the recordings of those conversations. I can't imagine what that must have been like.

"So, Adam, how was your day?"

"And, God, the Almighty, how was your day?"

Sorry, I just can't wrap my mind around it. But I do see this. Adam and Eve were so important to God that He wanted to spend time with them, apparently, everyday. Grab on to that. God, the Almighty, wanted to spend time everyday with two walking, talking piles of dirt!

What He made, He loved...deeply. He wanted to be with them, He wanted them to be with Him. And He made within them the capacity, ability and need to have fellowship with Him. That's where God started with them. And if we are going to get to the right destination in this life we must keep *starting at the right starting point.* God wants to fellowship us. He wants to listen to us and He wants us to listen to Him.

But then I think, *"Yeah, well, that was before they messed up. Once they chose to disobey Him, He was ticked off! He was hot! And He poured out His wrath on them and on all their kids. I don't want to get too close to Him because I know I have messed up and I am pretty sure I will mess up again."*

But wait a minute. Is this what really happened in the garden? Is that really the message this story teaches us? Or have we had this story, and the God at the heart of this story, misrepresented to us? What does this story actually teach us about *What God is really like* and *How He really feels about us*?

To answer those questions, we have to back up and ask some different questions about this story.

Asking The Right Questions

Question Number One

- ***Did God know they had sinned before He came into the garden?***

To answer this we must see that the Bible describes God as *"eternal, having no beginning or end".* He exists *"from everlasting to everlasting".* In human terms, He is timeless.

Though all human analogies fall terribly short of describing the Infinite God, it helps me to view God as existing above and beyond time. It is as if *He looks down upon time.* He sees the past, present and future all at the same time. He knows what *was*, what *is*, and what is *to come.*

Time was part of the creation. *"The evening and morning were the first day".* This creation of time was *"for signs and for seasons and for days and years..."* (Gen. 1) These are all delineations of time. Rev. 21 refers to a time when there will be more need for the sun and moon to mark the passing of time because we will exist with God eternally. There will be no need for time as we know it now.

I believe this is important if we are going to understand what happened in the garden...but you don't want to think about it too much. Our finite minds just cannot truly comprehend something so far beyond our time/space world. If we think about it too much, smoke might start coming out of our ears!

Let's just accept the divine reality that the all-knowing God, *to whom nothing is hidden* (Heb.4:13), knew what they had done before He came into the garden that day.

Which brings us to –

Question Number Two

– *What was the first thing God <u>did</u> after Adam and Eve sinned?*

We can only go on what the Genesis 3 text tells us. The first thing God did after they sinned?

He came into the garden to meet with them... just like every other day!

Think about what this says about God and His heart for them. Knowing what they had done, He apparently came into he garden in the cool of the day to fellowship them, *just like always*!

If I were God, I would have come into the garden, too...and I would have been hot! Come on, I gave them one commandment, just one! And they promptly broke it! If I were God, I would know that I was going to give Moses ten commandments, but I only gave them one and they broke the only one I gave them. Would I be angry? You bet.

And I would have had a lot to say to them when I got there. Probably something like, *"Yeah, you better hide because when I find you, you're gonna be in big trouble!"* That sounds appropriately parental. But is this the heart of God?

And this brings us to the next question –

Question Number Three

- *What was the first thing God <u>said</u> when He came into the garden?*

Again, we can only go by the information the Holy Spirit gave us. So what is the first thing the Bible tells us God said?

"Where are you?"

"Where are you???" Did God suddenly lose His omniscience? Did He suddenly go dumb? Did He not know exactly where they were hiding?

Of course, He did. He knew the precise tree they were hiding behind. He knew exactly what they had done and exactly where they were hiding. And He knew why they were hiding.

So why did He ask this strange question and what could this be telling us about *What God is really like* and *How He really feels about us*?

God Comes Into The Garden And Invites Them To Come To Him

This is amazing. This is huge! The Righteous Judge has the perfect opportunity to pour out wrath upon these ingrates or, at the very least, leave them to their new friend and advisor, the serpent.

But instead, He comes to them...*just like always*. He calls out to them, inviting them to come to Him for help.

He draws near to them

and invites them to draw near to Him.

In the New Testament we are told to *"Draw near to God and He will draw near to you"* (James 4:8). This declaration is frequently used to show that the responsibility is completely on us; we must make the first move.

But, in fact, this passage in James comes after thousands of years of examples of this faithful, loving God drawing near to sinful failures and continually giving them the invitation to come to Him for help. And we are consistently shown that judgment did come because He, indeed, is holy, righteous and just. But judgment came only after people deliberately chose to reject His free gift of help.

So here is a life-changing question –

Who makes the first move?

<u>He did.</u> <u>He does.</u> <u>*He always does!*</u>

He made the first move towards them in the garden. He made the first move towards them in Egypt. He made the first move towards them with each prophet He sent. He made the first move towards the world at the cross.

And His Spirit keeps making the first move towards us today. What He requires of us is to respond to His invitation by seeing *What He is really like* and *How He really feels about us!*

I know this is getting redundant and you may be thinking, "Alright, already. Enough". But I have become absolutely convinced that these two big questions, *What is God really like* and *How does He really feel about me*, are the most important questions of life. I am also convinced we must constantly have our minds renewed so we can stand in true faith and be empowered to answer them correctly in every season of our lives.

And, I am fully convinced that every attack of the enemy is directly aimed at getting us to miss the answer to these two questions. In fact, let me go one step further.

I have become fully convinced that how we answer these two questions will either set us free from fear...or fill us with it. Our answer will either wash us from shame...or overwhelm us with it. And our answer will either break the stranglehold

It's My Parents' Fault

of condemnation...or guarantee we can never be free of its confidence-killing effects.

Adam and Eve's faulty answer to these two important questions about God made them afraid and ashamed; and it made them draw back from the only One who could help them.

Why am I still so much like my distant parents?

Chapter Eleven

Draw Near or Draw Back

Let's review our important questions about Genesis 3.

1) Did God know they had sinned before He came into the garden?

Yes. And He came to them anyway.

2) What was the first thing God *did* after they sinned?

He came into the garden to fellowship them, *just like always*.

3) What was the first thing God *said* when He came into the garden?

"Where are you?" He was inviting them, *in their sin*, to come to Him for help. He had their cure but they had to come back into His Presence to get it.

These facts agree completely with the way God describes Himself in Exodus 34 –

> *"...full of mercy, full of compassion, always ready to forgive every manner of sin and transgression, keeping His love to thousands of generations to any who will love Him..."*

When we read it simply the way it is written for us, the truth comes clear. Both the Old Testament and New Testament show God is always moving toward people who fail. Then He invites them to respond by drawing near to Him for His cure.

This is what "*the faith*" referred to in the New Testament is all about; believing God's invitation and acting upon it by drawing near to Him in our failure and weakness.

Why Didn't They Draw Near To Him?

But if this is *What God is really like* and *How He really feels about us*, why did Adam and Eve hide from Him? Why didn't they draw near to Him in their failure?

The answer seems clear. God has now been misrepresented to them. They had begun to believe a lie. The most important lie they now believed was not about themselves, but about God. They now believed a lie about how He would react to their failure, a lie about how the Almighty *felt* about them now that they have sinned.

From the very first day of their existence, God had been their Creator, their Father and their Provider. All the evidence tells us He had been nothing but loving, caring and attentive to their needs. And, because we know He knew what they were going to do, we know His goodness wasn't based on them and their nature, but on Himself and His nature.

From the moment they began listening to the serpent, their belief about *What God is really like* and *How He really felt about them* began to change. They no longer knew God *as He really is*.

They had always been happy to hear His voice coming into the garden. But now when they hear Him coming, they are afraid, ashamed and condemned; so they hide. They are now hiding from the One they had always run to, the One who always loved and cared for them. They are hiding from the only one who can help them!

Genesis 3:8 says that when Adam and Eve heard the sound of the Lord walking in the garden they hid themselves from His *Presence*. When He calls to them and invites them to come to Him (*knowing exactly what they have done*), they now say,

> *"We heard the sound of You coming into the garden and we were afraid. We were ashamed and we hid from you".*

Afraid, ashamed, and hiding.

Fear, shame and condemnation.

These three things caused them to draw back instead of drawing near. Imagine this tragedy.

- The *Presence* they have always loved, they now fear.

- The *Presence* they have always run to, they now run from.

- The *Presence* that had always provided everything they needed, they now believe won't provide what they need most – forgiveness, acceptance and covering.

Our Nature or God's Nature

Our parents made the same mistake we make today. They began to believe God's love depended on their nature when it actually depends on His nature. And the revelation of His true nature is meant to draw us to Him.

Remember, God's declaration to Moses in Exodus 34 was in response to the failure of the people to obey. Paul understood this when he said to his spiritual son, Timothy, *"If we are faithless, He remains faithful, for He cannot deny Himself."* (2 Tim. 2:13)

God was clearly telling us that His nature remains the same and that His promise to remain compassionate, merciful and forgiving is in direct response to our inability to hear and obey.

His loving promise is in direct response to our inability!

Adam Had Another Choice He Could Have Made

The moment Adam realized what he had done, he chose to draw back from God's Presence. But he could have made another choice.

He could have cried out, *"Father, we have messed up. Please don't wait until this evening to come. We desperately need You to come right now!"*

That choice would have been *drawing near*. But fear, shame and condemnation caused him to *draw back*. And as Adam's kids, we choose to *draw back* for the same three reasons – *fear, shame and condemnation*.

Can Good Works Fix This?

Adam and Eve's thinking is so twisted from listening to the serpent that they now believe their problem is their nakedness.

*"I was afraid because I was **naked**; so I hid myself."*

One day, as I read this passage again, Adam's twisted thinking dawned on me when I asked myself the question, *"How long had they been naked?"*

Well, the whole time, of course. They had always been naked. God created Adam and Eve naked and it had never been a problem to Him. Genesis 2:25 says they were created naked and they were *not ashamed*. The animals weren't bothered by their nakedness. Their nakedness certainly didn't bother each other.

But sin has so twisted their thinking about God, they now believe their nakedness will bother Him and He won't want them in His Presence. So they decide to fix their problem by doing the *"good work"* of covering themselves. Based on what they now believe about God, this is a logical action...wrong, but logical.

Remember, they hid from His *Presence*. That is an important word. And now, they desperately want to get back into His *Presence*. But they are convinced that what is keeping them out of His *Presence* is their nakedness. So they make clothing out of the nearest, usable material; fig leaves. Surely, this good work, this hard work, this act of serious effort will fix their problem and allow them back into His Presence.

I can just imagine their thinking because I have become pretty much of an expert in this kind of religious logic.

"There has to be something we can do to fix this mess. We have disobeyed and now we are naked. Surely God doesn't want us in His presence in this condition. We have to do some good work to cover up our bad work. Look, fig leaves. They are soft and pliable, and they will cover our nakedness. Once we fix the mess we've made, maybe God will allow us back into His presence."

This seems so logical. In fact, it seems so logical it is either the direct or indirect subject of countless sermons designed to motivate people to straighten up and act right. I know, I have preached many of them.

But this is faulty logic and I was wrong. Far more importantly, it is completely unscriptural; it is biblically wrong, just plain wrong!

God's Brilliant Cure

Chapter Twelve

The Problem With Fig Leaves

I am sure fig leaves seemed like a good idea at the time. But think about it. Today, they're green, leafy and pliable. But in a day or two, they are brown, wilted and dried up. I bump them once and they crumble into little pieces...and I am naked all over again!

What a perfect example of good works done out of a motive of fear and guilt. Good works done in human effort for the wrong motives don't cure anything...and they never truly last.

This is the same kind of thinking that says, *"I know I really messed up. I know I sinned. I should know better by now, but I still messed up. And I know the holy God doesn't want me in His presence like this. So here's what I am going to do.*

God, I promise I will never act like that again. No, I really mean it this time, I promise. And to prove I really mean it this time, instead of reading five chapters a day, now I am going to read ten.

I know you don't want me in Your Presence when I mess up like this, but if I read ten chapters a day, surely that will fix it so I can come back into Your Presence, right?"

Maybe for you, it's not ten chapters. Perhaps it's getting up earlier so you can pray longer. Or sacrificing something you enjoy so you can give more to missions. Or maybe it's being really, really mad at yourself to prove you really mean it this time.

But our good works have the same problem as Adam's fig leaves; they don't cure anything and they don't last. Our promises never do. Our promises, made out of our fear or shame, depend on our ability. And our ability will always fall short and our failure will steal our faith to take God at His word and depend on Him to do His work *in* and *through* us. God always wants to do *in* and *through* us what we cannot possibly do for ourselves. This is what He is really like!

God's Cure Is In His Presence

Since his nakedness didn't bother anyone else, the only possible reason Adam would have for covering himself was to get back into God's Presence. Any time we do good works because we feel guilty that we haven't lived perfectly, we fall into the same trap Adam fell into –

Good Works Can Never Earn God's Presence.

We cannot earn, by our good works, what God wants to give us as a free gift. God fully understood Adam's twisted thinking and He had the solution for Adam's perceived problem. And before this story is over, He demonstrates His cure for the problem Adam thought he had and He declares His eternal cure for Adam's *real problem*.

Let's go back to the garden.

"The LORD God made garments of skin for Adam and his wife, and clothed them."

(Gen. 3:21)

God understands what is troubling Adam and, in love, He brushes aside their feeble, temporary effort to fix themselves. He doesn't rebuke them for the fig leaves. He doesn't curse them for trying to fix their problem.

He just brushes away their failing efforts, kills an animal and makes durable, long-lasting coverings for them. He doesn't want them to feel ashamed any longer. But the Almighty God wants to be the One who fixes this problem for them and the cure can only come in His Presence.

This Is Not A *"Do-It-Yourself"* Project

God did not want Adam and Eve to fix this problem for themselves. God wanted to fix it for them. This was never intended to be a *"do-it-yourself"* project.

Can you imagine God looking at Adam clothed in dry, crumbling fig leaves? He is surrounded by animals that are reproducing very well and yet he chooses to make coverings out of leaves? Adam could have easily skinned one of those many animals and made durable clothing for himself. But leaves seemed like a better idea to him??? God must have surely thought He created Adam with a better brain than that!

But God doesn't tell Adam how to cover himself. God wants to do the work for him. He wants to take care of Adam, Himself. He wants to do this for the creation He loves.

Instead of God teaching Adam how to do it for himself, God wants to do it for him. He wanted them to get their solution from Him. This was never intended to be a "*do-it-yourself*" project but a "*do-it-**to**-me*" work that God wants to do ***in*** and ***through*** us.

*(See **God's Brilliant Plan** for a full discussion of this plan for Christ to live His life in and through us)*

Adam and Eve had to come back into in His Presence to get His solution. They couldn't fix themselves and *earn* their way back into His Presence. To get His cure for their problem, they had to draw near to Him...first. They had to come back into His Presence...first!

Please hear this conversation between God and Adam because I know it has changed my life forever.

"Adam, where are you?"

"We have drawn back from You because we have messed up."

"Adam, come here to Me and let me fix this."

*"But we can't draw near to You yet, because we have **really** messed up."*

"That's the very reason why you need to come to Me, because I want to fix this for you. So, Adam, come here."

They drag themselves out of hiding and stand, again, in His Presence. And the Righteous, Holy God covers their sin by killing one of His creatures and clothing them, Himself. Their answer was in His Presence. The cure for their well-deserved fear, shame and condemnation could only be found there, standing beside Him...in His Presence.

The Real Problem And The Real Promise

Of course, their real problem was an eternal one. But God had the cure for that one, too. God now speaks to the serpent (*a metaphor for the devil*) so that Adam and Eve can hear the promise.

> *"From now on, you and the woman will be enemies, and your offspring and her offspring will be enemies.* ***He will crush your head****, and you will strike his heel."*

(Gen. 3:15 NLT)

Remember, Jesus is the substance that fulfils every shadow in the Old Testament. Here is the of the first *shadows* of the *substance* that was promised. A seed (*Jesus*) would come through the woman and He would fulfill every promise. Paradise Lost will be Paradise Restored with the full, unveiled Presence of God.

Every human being who has ever put their hope in the Promised Seed receives the promise that He, the second Adam, will come and crush the head of the one who has troubled us throughout the ages. That promise was fulfilled at the cross and will be fully realized at His second coming.

Adam's disobedience was not a *"problem"* for God because He already had the cure for them. But to get God's cure Adam had to come back into His presence just as he was– *fearful, ashamed and feeling condemned.* He had to draw near to God and let God do the cure *for* him; let Him do the cure *to* him.

And the way to receive the Father's cure hasn't changed. Just like my original parents, Adam and Eve, I must choose to overcome my fear by believing what God says about Himself and I must choose to draw near to Him.

I can, and must, choose to believe *What God is really like* and *How He really feels about me*...and draw near to Him!

But, wait a minute. I know God is completely holy and I am certainly not. How can someone as unholy as me come into the Presence of a holy God?

Maybe if I work harder and make myself more holy, He will reward me with more of His Presence.

Maybe…but, maybe not.

Chapter Thirteen

Is God's Presence A Reward For Holy Behavior?

OK, this is one of those statements which cause some of my more *"holy"* friends to really worry about me. And I understand why.

"God's Presence is <u>not</u> a reward for holy behavior."

Depending on your religious background, this can sound almost like heresy. I know it sounded like that to me for many years. Depending on the way you view God, this can certainly sound like I am saying, *"God is so loving, merciful and good that our unholiness doesn't really matter"*.

I am not saying that at all. But I can understand why some might think I am. What I am saying is this: there is great danger in thinking that the cause of something is actually the effect of it; or that the source of something is actually the result of it. We must ask these questions –

> *Do I make myself holy so I can encounter the Holy God? Or does encountering the Holy God make me holy?*
>
> *Which is the cause and which is the effect?*
>
> *Which is the source and which is the result?*

I know how I used to think –

> *"Of course, holy behavior allows me to experience more of God's holy presence. God does reward us with more of His holy presence when we discipline ourselves unto godliness. God cannot abide unholiness. Unholiness cannot come into His Presence. So the more holy I make myself, the more good works I do, the better I behave, the more He will reward me with His Presence, right?"*

No. Sorry. It just can't happen. When I believed those things, for all those years, I was wrong; and I was miserable. I was wrong because it violates everything God says about Himself. It contradicts everything the Bible says He wants to do *for* us, *to* us and *in* us. And there is just too much scriptural evidence that tells us God does not act like that.

If your background is anything like mine, what you have just read might sound pretty extreme, but please don't put this book down yet. Since you have obviously read this far, let me give you the punch line now. I will attempt to prove the extreme importance of understanding and living in the reality of these next, seemingly brash statements.

<u>Here is the eternal truth that can set us free –</u>

God's Presence is not the reward for holiness...

God's Presence is the *means* to holiness.

God's Presence is not the reward for good behavior...

Good behavior is a *result* of being in God's Presence.

You can't get to know God better by acting better...

You will act better as you get to *know* God better.

You can't make yourself more holy so He will give you more of His Presence...

You experience more of His Presence and He *makes* you holier in the process.

Sounds good, but is this is what the Bible actually teaches? We must not lean on our own logic here. We must *"Trust in the LORD with all your heart and do not lean on your own understanding."* (Pro. 3:5)

In the following pages we are going to examine numerous examples to see if this is true. But we have to start back in the garden.

What is God Really Like?

The serpent begins his attack by questioning the heart and nature of God. He told them God was not telling them the truth and He was actually keeping something good and important from them.

> *The serpent said to the woman, "You surely will not die! For God knows that in the day you eat from it your eyes will be opened, and you will be like God, knowing good and evil."*
>
> (Gen. 3:4-5)

By telling them that God was withholding something good and important from them, the serpent strikes at the heart of *What God is really like* and *He really feels about you.*

They began to question whether God was really like they thought He was. Instead of waiting until God came into the garden that afternoon and asking Him if this was true, they began to believe God may not be as good as they thought He was. So they made a judgment in their own wisdom and then acted on the judgment they made about God's nature and heart.

> "He **is** withholding something good and important from us. So we will make our own decision. We can see with our own eyes that the fruit is good and important because it will make us wise; we can see that it will make us like God."

The immediate result in Adam and Eve was exactly what the serpent said would happen. Their eyes were opened. But they didn't see God more clearly. In fact, they lost sight of *What He was really like* and *How He really felt about them*.

Their eyes were actually closed to God. But they were opened to see...*themselves*. They suddenly became *self-aware* and lost their God-awareness. And their newly found self-awareness brought some other new things into their consciousness – *fear, shame and condemnation*.

"Who Told You That?"

When God comes into the garden, Adam says, *"We were afraid of You and we were ashamed for You to see us like this. So we hid from Your Presence and tried to fix ourselves."*

God already knows everything they have done. He already knows exactly what's happened. But it is important for Adam to understand what has happened. So God asks them the critical question.

> *"And He said, '**Who told you that** you were naked?'"*
>
> (Gen. 3:11)

Adam has just confessed that he was *afraid, ashamed and condemned*. And God's response is –

"Who told you that?"

"Who have you been listening to?"

"You didn't get those ideas from Me."

What does this say about God? What does this say about His nature and His heart for them?

Knowing what they have done, He comes to them. Knowing what they have done, He calls to them, inviting them to come to Him. Now He shows them that the fear, shame and condemnation they feel did not come from Him.

He shows them that what comes from Him is the invitation to the cure. Out of His love and care for them, He covers their shame, restores their relationship with Him and gives them the eternal promise that through the coming "*Seed*" they can live in right relationship with Him forever. They couldn't earn their way back into His Presence. He was giving it as a gift for their healing.

Whenever I feel afraid that my behavior will make God not want me near Him, ***I must ask myself***, *"Who told me that?"*

Whenever I feel ashamed of my failure and feel God may no longer want me near Him, *I must ask myself*, *"Who told me that?"*

Whenever something goes wrong and I feel condemned thinking God is now punishing me for not being all I should be or doing all I should do, *I must ask myself*, *"Who told me that?"*

Then I must choose to believe the truth; those feelings and thoughts did not come from God. What actually does come from God is the same message He gave to Adam, *"I understand your weakness. Now come to me for the cure".*

Isn't this completely consistent with the declaration of our New Covenant High Priest and His invitation to us?

> *"This High Priest of ours understands our weaknesses... **So let us come boldly** to the throne of our gracious God. There we will receive his mercy, and we will find grace to help us when we need it."*
>
> (Heb. 4:15-16 NLT)

We are faced with the same choice God gave Adam –

Draw Near or Draw Back

Earning A Visit To The Doctor

The Bible frequently refers to our relationship with God in medical terms. He is the *"balm of Gilead"*, He will *"anoint our eyes with salve"*, He is *"Jehovah Rapha, our Healer"*.

We refer to Jesus as the Great Physician. When the Pharisees complained that Jesus spent too much time with unrighteous people, He said, *"It is not those who are healthy who need a physician, but those who are sick; I did not come to call the righteous, but sinners."* (Mark 2:17)

Clearly, God's heart is to invite those who are sick to come to Him, in their sickness, and receive His cure. Adam and Eve were clearly *"sick"* with sin; and their condition filled them with fear, shame and condemnation. So God invites them to come to Him and be healed. They couldn't heal themselves and earn a place back in His Presence. They had to come back into His Presence, with their sickness, and receive His cure.

To say that God's Presence is a reward for holy behavior is the same as saying getting in to see the doctor is a reward for getting well. A doctor's visit is supposed to be the **means** of getting well. We not confuse the source with the result. We must not confuse the cause with the effect.

Imagine I call my doctor's office and get the scheduling nurse.

"Hi, I would like to make an appointment to see the doctor."

"I can take care of that, Mr. Drake. Now, what's the problem?"

"Oh, nothing now. I'm good now."

"What do you mean, 'nothing is wrong, now?'"

"Well, two weeks ago I was really sick. But I'm good now."

"Mr. Drake, why didn't you come to see the doctor two weeks ago?"

"Oh, I was much too embarrassed for the doctor to see me like that! But I'm good now, so I would like to see the doctor."

Too embarrassed for the doctor to see me like that? How absurd. The whole purpose of going to see the doctor is so he can give me a cure while I am still sick. No one would act like that.

Really? Isn't that what we do every time we feel too ashamed to draw near and worship Him when we know we have really messed up?

Isn't that what convinces us we don't deserve to enter in, enjoy His Presence and receive His cure unless we have behaved exactly as a Christian should act? Isn't that what makes us feel we don't have the right to enter in because we don't deserve it?

This kind of wrong thinking is exactly what made Adam hide in fear and shame from the very Presence that came to heal him. He sinned, he failed, and then he judged God wrongly. But God came and drew Adam back into His

Presence to heal him of his sin, wash him of his fear and cover his shame.

We will be tormented with Adam's destructive way of thinking as long as we mistakenly believe God's presence is a reward for good behavior. We must let the Word and the Spirit wash our conscience and renew our minds so we can see that God's presence is medicine for what plagues us.

God's presence is _not_ the reward for holiness...

God's Presence is the _means_ to holiness.

God's presence is not the reward for good behavior...

Good behavior is a _result_ of being in God's presence.

You can't get to know God better by acting better...

You will _act_ better as you get to _know_ God better.

But I have been around long enough to know you can't build a doctrine on just one story. So the question remains, does the Bible actually teach that we are supposed to *draw near to the Holy God in our unholy failure*?

Chapter Fourteen

Come Here And Be Changed

"In the year King Uzziah died, I saw the Lord."

(Is. 6:1)

With these simple words, Isaiah begins to describe one of the most amazing, dramatic and life-changing encounters with God you will ever read.

I am one who believes in human encounters with the Living God. I have had several weird, wonderful, *"take-your-breath-away"* encounters with God over the years. I can't explain them. I can't tell you how to make them happen. I can't even tell you the reason why most of them occurred. And I have lived long enough to be very skeptical of any preacher/teacher who says they can tell you when, where, why or how to make them happen.

But this I know, for sure; every encounter left me changed. Whether it came in a still, small, whispering inner voice as I meditated on a passage of scripture or in a mighty, rushing, spiritual wind that shook me deep inside and left me breathless; *each encounter changed me.*

And most of them left me changed in ways that I often didn't recognize until days, months or even years later. And more often than not, other people noticed the change before I did. (*My wife usually sees the change sooner than I do.*)

And being changed is what encountering God is all about. Not blessing, though you may be blessed as a result. Not power, although you may feel more power in your life afterwards. And certainly, not a great story you can boast about in the next meeting. In fact, I suspect that some of the stories we charismatics tell when trying to impress others with our spirituality are, if not completely fabricated, at least, seriously exaggerated to make us look better.

Paul Had The Best Story But He Wouldn't Tell

Remember this; when Paul had what is arguably the most divine encounters recorded in the New Testament where he was caught up into third heaven, into the very presence of God, he refused to tell the specifics of what happened. In fact, he said that some things are not supposed to be told.

*'I was caught up into the third heaven fourteen years ago. Whether my body was there or just my spirit, I don't know; only God knows. But I do know that I was caught up into paradise and heard things so astounding that **they cannot be told**. That experience is something worth boasting about, but I am not going to do it. I am going to boast only about my*

weaknesses. I have plenty to boast about and would be no fool in doing it, because I would be telling the truth. But I won't do it."

(2 Cor. 12:2-60 NLT)

I sometimes wonder how Paul's experience relates to the rash of current stories of how *"I spent so many minutes in heaven"* or *"what I learned when I visited hell"*. After reading a few of these stories, I have serious questions about how some of them line up with the written Word. My advice is: be careful what you read…even what you read here.

Paul goes on to say that the real importance of that divine encounter was that he realized his weakness; he saw what was wrong with him and how God wanted to transform him. The important result for Paul was that the power of God's grace worked in and through him more than ever. He was changed.

Being changed is what genuine encounters are supposed to produce. We are supposed to be *"growing in the knowledge of Him"* and being changed by that process. This is God's cure; His brilliant cure for our dilemma. He wants to change us when we cannot change ourselves.

What Happens to Unholy People In God's Holy Presence?

When we looked at the story of what happened in the garden, we tried to read and understand it simply as it was written. As we began, we asked ourselves the question, *"How does God feel about people who really mess up?"*

God's Brilliant Cure

As we read Isaiah's story, we need to ask ourselves, *"What happens to unholy people when they come into God's Holy Presence?"*

As we read Isaiah's account, watch the progression from the glory and *goose bumps* of what he sees, to the transformation that is done to him and within him. God's Brilliant Cure!

> *In the year King Uzziah died, I saw the Lord. He was sitting on a lofty throne, and the train of his robe filled the Temple. Hovering around him were mighty seraphim, each with six wings. With two wings they covered their faces, with two they covered their feet, and with the remaining two they flew. In a great chorus they sang, "Holy, holy, holy is the LORD Almighty! The whole earth is filled with his glory!" The glorious singing shook the Temple to its foundations, and the entire sanctuary was filled with smoke.*
>
> *Then I said, "My destruction is sealed, for I am a sinful man and a member of a sinful race. Yet I have seen the King, the LORD Almighty!"*
>
> *Then one of the seraphim flew over to the altar, and he picked up a burning coal with a pair of tongs. He touched my lips with it and said, "See, this coal has touched your lips. Now your guilt is removed, and your sins are forgiven."*
>
> (Isa. 6:1-7) NLT

The heavens open and Isaiah sees into the very throne room of the Almighty God. The Infinite One who sits upon the throne is the focus of everything. The glory of the Glorious One covers everything. The majesty of the Mighty One has overwhelmed everything. This story is utterly drenched in the holiness of the Most Holy One.

This is a scene Steven Spielberg and George Lucas couldn't even come close to recreating on a 3D movie screen. Bizarre, angelic creatures with multiple wings are flying back and forth above the throne. Their very purpose is to continually declare holiness: *"Holy, Holy, Holy is the Lord!"*

Remember our key question – *"What happens to unholy people in the presence of the Most Holy God?"* And this story is all about the absolute holiness of God and the admitted unholiness of a man in His Presence.

The angelic beings cry out, *"The whole Earth is filled with His Glory"*, and just that declaration causes everything to tremble and shake. Smoke, or the glory cloud of God's holy presence, fills the temple. And Isaiah is watching it all unfold before his very eyes.

"My Destruction Is Sealed"

If there was ever a time for sinful, fragile flesh to be utterly consumed by the perfectness of the Holy God, this would be the time. If there was ever a time for the fire of God to devour sinful humanity, now would be the time.

And indeed, as he witnesses the unveiling of the holiness of God, Isaiah realizes something terrifying about himself; he is desperately unholy; "*I am unclean*". And based on the way he viewed the Holy God, he thought he knew what would logically come next.

"My destruction is sealed, for I am a sinful man".

This was the obvious conclusion based on how Isaiah was taught to answer the questions, *What is God really like* and *How does He really feel about me.* And the clear results of his answers were fear, shame and condemnation.

"I am a dead man. It's over for me. I am in the presence of the Holy Judge and my unholiness will bring His immediate wrath. I shouldn't be here, I don't deserve to be here, I am undone and, soon, I will be dead."

If God Was Like I Thought He Was

I have to be honest. Even standing on the New Testament side of the demonstration of God's unconditional love through the cross, I have had trouble with this story for years. If God was really like I thought He was, this is the way the story would have unfolded.

Isaiah must have been praying and fasting for weeks. Clearly, he was seeking God more than any other Israelite. He must have been telling God what an awful worm he knew he was and making serious promises to God that he was going to try harder and be better. So God rewarded him with a glimpse into heaven.

Isaiah saw the Lord as his reward for trying so hard to be so holy. He saw the glory of God, the majesty of His throne room and the awesomeness of the angelic creatures. And he confessed how unworthy he was to even be in God's presence.

Then, if God was like I thought He was, He would have said, *"Isaiah, I am so glad you finally realize how awful you are. Now get out of My Presence, go away and make yourself worthy. You know that nothing unholy can be in My Presence. Build an altar and burn the unholiness out of your life. Burn up the things that are the most important to you and prove to Me how serious you really are. And if I think you have done enough to make yourself worthy, I may allow you to come into My Presence again."*

And because God is so holy and Isaiah was not, God would use fear, shame and condemnation to motivate Isaiah to clean himself up. But that is not how this story unfolds.

In fact, it turns out to be quite the opposite.

Chapter Fifteen

What Happens To Unholy People In God's Holy Presence

There is no indication that Isaiah did anything special to earn this encounter with God. In fact, it seems he was in despair because the king had recently died. His leader, protector and provider was now gone. He may well have been feeling very helpless and utterly hopeless.

There is no indication that Isaiah drew near to God of his own volition. Since Isaiah deeply feared being destroyed, there is clear indication that Isaiah was afraid to draw near to this *"great and terrible"* God.

Clearly, Isaiah's view of God was not the same as God's description of Himself in Exodus 34. His fear that the Holy Judge would destroy him because of his unholiness seems to reveal that Isaiah suffered from the same wrong view of God as the rest of the people. So God moved toward him. God drew near to him.

Allow me some literary license as I retell what happened to this sincere, but unclean man as he stood in the Presence of the Most Holy God.

God knew all about Isaiah's lack of holiness and He drew him into His Holy Presence anyway. Actually, God drew Isaiah into His Holy Presence *because* he was unholy.

God had a plan and it was a ***brilliant plan***. God had Isaiah's cure and it was a ***brilliant cure***. Brilliant, because God provided all the elements needed for this amazing cure. But I saiah had a choice to make. To get God's cure Isaiah had to come back into God's Presence. So God drew him in.

How Unholy Am I?

Isaiah didn't realize the depth of his unholiness until he stood in the Presence of the Holy God. It was being in God's Presence that caused Isaiah to see himself and see his desperate need of a cure.

Isaiah confesses the truth about himself, *"I realize I am unclean because I have seen the King"*. As he beheld the glory of the Most Holy God he saw how desperately he needed to be changed.

But the realization of his unholiness didn't get him kicked out of the throne room. Instead, God invites him to stay in His presence so He can work His plan *for* him, *to* him and *in* him. In His Presence, the Holy God implements His brilliant cure for Isaiah's unholiness.

Listen To God's Response To Isaiah's Confession

> *"Isaiah, I am glad you finally realize the great difference between you and Me. Now, stay right where you are, here in my Presence. Keep your eyes on Me. Don't let your unworthiness make you draw back. It's important that you see your sin and admit it, but don't let it corrupt your view of Me. Don't let self-awareness cause you to draw back from Me. Stay aware of Me and my heart for you. Stay right here, in my Presence, and let me do a cleansing work **for** you, **to** you and **in** you."*

God's Altar Or Mine

God now says to an angel, *"It's time for you to do your job"*. The angel flies to God's altar and uses tongs to pick up a burning coal. Notice this is God's altar, not an altar Isaiah built.

I have built many *"altars of promises and sacrifice"* hoping they would somehow change me. They never did because my promises don't have real, transforming power. And if they did, I would want all the credit and that would ruin whatever good was done. But God's promises, in God's presence, have true, transforming power!

Throughout the Bible people built altars to remember something God did *for* them. Victories He won for them when they didn't have the power to win for themselves. Help He provided for them when they couldn't provide help for themselves. God's description of Himself in Exodus 34 shows Him to be a God who delights in doing for us what we cannot possibly do for ourselves.

Even the altar Abraham built to sacrifice Isaac upon became a memorial to the fact that God drew near to him and did for Abraham what Abraham could not do for himself.

This story of Abraham offering his only son is so often taught as an example of how we must pay the ultimate price and prove to God we are truly serious. I used to teach that way. But in fact, this story of Abraham and Isaac is a great story of what He wants to do *for* us.

Remember, the Bible is written in human terms. It is written in a way human beings can, at least, begin to understand the indescribable God. God already knew Abraham's heart completely. It was Abraham who needed to know his own heart and then see God as the One who would provide all he needed; including the perfect sacrifice.

This is the faith of Abraham that Paul tells us we must have. It is a faith that convinces us that God's heart and nature wants to do for us what we cannot possibly do for ourselves. This is the result of coming to know *What God is really like* and *How He really feels about us.*

God's Cleansing Fire

Let's go back into the heavenly holy place where Isaiah has just realized how unholy he really is. God sends His angel to pick up a burning coal from His altar. The angel flies to where Isaiah is still standing, in God's Presence, and touches his lips. Then the angel tells Isaiah what was just done *for* him, *to* him and *in* him.

> "See, this coal has touched your lips. Now your guilt is removed, and your sins are forgiven."
>
> (Isa. 6:7 NLT)

In my struggle to understand how I can ever live free of fear, shame and condemnation, understanding the simple truths in these amazing stories gives me tremendous hope!

I have built so many fires over the years hoping I could somehow burn the ungodliness out of my life; fires of rededication and recommitment, fires of promises and sacrifices. All the while, hoping with all my heart that my fire would somehow change me, only to be disappointed again and again with the lack of permanent change.

But I have also had those moments where I knew that for some reason beyond myself, when I least deserved it, God had drawn me into His Presence. And in His Presence, a cleansing fire came and something changed within me. I didn't earn it and I couldn't do anything to deserve it, but I knew I had been touched by the cleansing fire of God and I was different.

Isaiah couldn't take any credit for the transformation that happened within him but he knew he was different. The Holy Presence he thought would kill him actually cured him.

You and I need to hear that again.

The Holy Presence Isaiah thought would kill him…actually cured him!

Grab on to this amazing truth because it will keep curing you of your fear, shame and condemnation!

This Is All God's Idea

It was God's idea, God's Presence, God's invitation, God's altar and God's fire that cleansed Isaiah from fear, shame and condemnation. It was all God's idea. It was God's cure, done God's way. God did the work. God gets the credit for the cleansing and Isaiah reaps the benefit of being made clean. What a Brilliant Cure!

It was God's idea to draw Adam and Eve back into His Presence to overcome their newly found fear of Him. It was God's idea to kill an animal and cover the shame they now felt in His Presence. And it was God's idea to give them the promise of the coming Seed who would take the curse upon Himself so they, and all their children who would choose to believe the same promise, would be free from fear, shame and condemnation forever!

God's presence was not a reward for Adam's holiness; it was the cure for his unholiness. God's Presence was not a reward for Isaiah's cleanliness. It was the cure for his uncleanness. And what a Brilliant Cure it was!

I wonder if I might be able to get that kind of cure.

Chapter Sixteen

A Wee Little Man Gets God's Cure

I didn't grow up sitting on little painted chairs in Sunday School being taught the stories of the Bible so I didn't learn the story of Zacchaeus until later in life. But it wasn't until my view of the heart and nature of God radically changed that I was able to see the simple, life-changing truth in this story.

Zacchaeus was hated by many of his fellow Jews because he took a job as a tax collector working for Rome. Tax collectors were given a quota based on the number of people living in their area. It was common in that day for tax collectors to deceive the people into thinking the tax was higher than it actually was and then keeping the extra for themselves. They were viewed as traitors to their people.

Zacchaeus was a small man, or as the Sunday School song goes, *"a wee little man was he"*. He heard stories about Jesus and wanted to see him. But because of his small size and the way most people felt about him, he never got close enough to see what was going on. So he climbed up a tree.

When Jesus came by, he looked up at Zacchaeus and called him by name. "Zacchaeus!" he said. "Quick, come down! For I must be a guest in your home today." Zacchaeus quickly climbed down and took Jesus to his house in great excitement and joy.

But the crowds were displeased. "He has gone to be the guest of a notorious sinner," they grumbled.

Meanwhile, Zacchaeus stood there and said to the Lord, "I will give half my wealth to the poor, Lord, and if I have overcharged people on their taxes, I will give them back four times as much!"

Jesus responded, "Salvation has come to this home today, for this man has shown himself to be a son of Abraham. And I, the Son of Man, have come to seek and save those like him who are lost."

(Luke 19:1-10 NLT)

What Does This Tell Us About How God Feels?

When we begin to seriously ask ourselves the questions, *What is God really like* and *How does He really feel about me*, we find stories like this throughout the Bible and they are filled with important clues.

Did Jesus know what kind of man Zacchaeus was before they met? Of course, He even knew his name.

Did Jesus wait for Zacchaeus to repent and become a good man before He allowed him into His presence?

No. Just the opposite happened. Before Zacchaeus gave any indication of wanting to change, Jesus said, *"I must come to your house today."*

Did Jesus give a teaching on the sin of overcharging people on their taxes? We have no indication of that.

What we are told is that just being in the Presence of Jesus did something to Zacchaeus' heart and he was changed. There was something about the holy Presence of Jesus that changed the hearts of any who wanted to be changed.

There is something awesome about the holy Presence of the Holy God; He transforms any unholy people who exercise just enough faith to draw near to Him. I am learning to exercise just enough faith to draw near to Him, over and over again!

And I am learning a great truth by drawing near. His Presence still changes any who want to be changed today for He is the same *"yesterday, today and forever!"* (Heb.13:8)

The Story Should Have Gone Like This

If God was really like I thought He was, the story should have gone like this.

> *Jesus had been preaching about the sin of cheating people and how angry that makes God. At the end of His message He said, "Let every head be bowed and every eye closed and no one looking around. If you know you are a sinner, if you know you have angered God by your disobedience, if you are willing to*

confess every filthy sin and promise God you are never going to act that way again, then I want you come forward and renounce your old way of life. Then God will love you and bless you. Then you will have a right to come into the Father's Holy Presence and I may go home with one of you and have supper in your house.

I fully understand that by writing that last paragraph I run a great risk of sounding like I think sin doesn't matter and that confession and repentance are not important. But nothing could be further from the truth.

I am saying that Jesus, knowing the power of His Presence, initiated the encounter; He invited Zacchaeus to draw near to Him, just as he was. And it was in His Presence that Zacchaeus' heart was transformed.

Zacchaeus didn't earn Jesus' presence by changing himself. He was changed by coming into His Presence; by drawing near to Him for His cure.

God's Presence Doesn't Change Everyone

To be clear, the Presence of God does not change everyone. The Pharisees experienced the same Presence of Jesus that Zacchaeus did but they hardened their hearts and they stopped up their ears so they wouldn't hear the truth about themselves.

Being in Jesus' presence caused Zacchaeus to see the truth about himself and he was changed. But to receive this

Brilliant Cure of transformation he had to admit the truth he saw about himself.

Israel experienced the Presence of God in the wilderness on a daily basis and in a variety of different ways. Yet, most of that generation refused to believe *What God was really like* and *How He really felt about them*. And most of them hardened their hearts and died in their unbelief.

It was their choice to not put their faith in the God who constantly revealed Himself as being *"full of compassion, abounding in lovingkindness, always willing to forgive every manner of sin and transgression"*. God gave them the evidence and the ability to believe. But they chose not to.

Making A Different Choice

The Pharisees saw the same evidence and many chose to remain in hardhearted unbelief. Adam made a different choice. Isaiah made a different choice. Zacchaeus made a different choice.

You and I are faced with the same two choices; draw near or draw back.

I have to look at the evidence of the Word, choose to believe *What God is really like* and *How He really feels about me;* and draw near to Him. And I have to keep making this choice every time trouble comes and I am tempted to doubt His nature and His heart towards me... and draw back.

But I have a second choice I must also make. And I must continue to make this choice every time I fall short of His image.

I must choose to face the hard truth about myself; my weakness, my failure, my sin. And if I want to be changed, I have to freely admit the truth about myself and draw near to God.

I want to be truthful and transparent before God but that seems so hard to do. I am afraid of what might happen if I admit the truth. Yet, I know if I don't, I will never be changed.

Clearly, I need help!

Chapter Seventeen

Facing The Hard Truth About Myself

Israel experienced the Presence of God in amazing ways and yet many of them were not changed. The Pharisees had the Son in their midst doing miracles and fulfilling the very prophecies they spent their lives studying, and yet, many of them were not changed.

Many of those who were healed by Jesus, and ate the miracle loaves and fishes, left Him and some helped crucify Him. And certainly, many of us have experienced genuine encounters with God, and yet, remained unchanged.

This happened then, and happens now, because of a crucial element God has built into our relationship with Him. At the end of the previous chapter we said there are two choices we must make.

The first choice is what we believe about God –

Will we choose to believe He is what He describes Himself to be and will we choose to believe He feels about us the way He says He does?

The second choice is what we believe about ourselves –

Will we choose to face the hard truth about ourselves and admit it to the Heavenly Doctor?

The questions God asked of Adam in the garden are the same questions that are critical for us in our search for freedom from fear, shame and condemnation.

Listen Again To The Questions

<u>Where are you?</u> (Gen. 3:9)

This was a direct invitation for Adam to come back into God's presence, in his sinful condition, so God could give him the cure. By inviting Adam back into His Presence, in his sin, God was not ignoring or excusing Adam's sin; He wanted to cure it for him.

<u>Who told you that?</u> (Gen. 3:11)

Adam had to see that what he now believed about God produced fear, shame and condemnation and these feelings did not come from God but from the *"accuser"* (Rev. 12:10), *"the father of lies"* (John 8:44). Adam couldn't change what he now believed unless he changed who he was listening to.

Listen to that again –

Adam couldn't change what he now believed, unless he changed who he was listening to.

Adam and Eve ate of the fruit hoping it would give them the ability to decide for themselves what was good and evil. Instead, their thinking was now influenced and perverted by the enemy. And human logic was born.

Face The Hard Truth And Admit It

I said earlier that I used to fear that this kind of thinking would somehow lead to "*loose living*" and carnal behavior because it sounds like I am saying Adam's sin didn't matter. But the third question God asks them shows that their sin, and their admission of it, was extremely important.

<u>What have you done?</u> (Gen.3:13)

Before God could free them from their fear, cover their shame and wash them from their feelings of condemnation, they had to admit what they had done. This willingness to admit the truth about themselves was absolutely essential to receive God's cure.

> *Before Isaiah could be cleansed by the fire of God, he had to admit that he was an unclean man.*
>
> *Before Zacchaeus could get free from his greed and dishonesty, he had to admit that he was a cheater.*

But these admissions did not <u>*earn*</u> their way into God's presence. It was being in God's presence that enabled them to see the truth about themselves and empowered them to admit it. They drew near instead of drawing back.

I Am Starting To See It Differently

When I saw this it changed my life. I no longer saw God's intimate, tangible Presence as a reward I had to work hard to earn. I no longer saw God's intimate, tangible Presence as a fearful place of punishment for my sin. I began on my journey of seeing God's Presence as the place of healing; a place of change and transformation. I started to see, and experience, God's Holy Presence as the medicine for my cure.

God's Presence is curative…

If we will tell the truth about ourselves!

God's Holiness is medicinal…

If we admit the truth about ourselves!

A Faulty View Causes Misunderstanding

If we start at the wrong starting point, we will always end up at the wrong destination. If we read Bible stories with the wrong view of God, we will misunderstand most of what we read.

For years I have read the Bible with glasses that were colored by a misrepresentation of God's nature and heart. Rather than reading the Bible to discover what God says about

Himself, I read the Bible with a preconceived belief about God. Then I interpreted what I read through my faulty view of Him, His nature and His heart for me.

And no one else is to blame for my faulty vision but me, because the Spirit of Truth has always been ready to guide me into a true understanding. But I am now on a journey into knowing Him *as He really is*. I am not there yet, and won't fully arrive in this life, but I am on the journey.

These Stories Troubled Me

One of the many stories that have troubled me for years is found in Matthew 15.

> *Jesus then left Galilee and went north to the region of Tyre and Sidon. A Gentile woman who lived there came to him, pleading, "Have mercy on me, O Lord, Son of David! For my daughter has a demon in her, and it is severely tormenting her."*
>
> *But Jesus gave her no reply — not even a word. Then his disciples urged him to send her away. "Tell her to leave," they said. "She is bothering us with all her begging."*
>
> *Then he said to the woman, "I was sent only to help the people of Israel – God's lost sheep – not the Gentiles." But she came and worshiped him and pleaded again, "Lord, help me!"*
>
> *"It isn't right to take food from the children and throw it to the dogs," he said. "Yes, Lord," she*

replied, *"but even dogs are permitted to eat crumbs that fall beneath their master's table."*

"Woman", Jesus said to her, "your faith is great. Your request is granted." And her daughter was instantly healed.

(Matt. 15:21-28 NLT)

This is one of many stories we are bound to misunderstand unless we know the context and who the players are. And it's easy to misunderstand, as the disciples did, because Jesus sounds so rude to this desperate lady.

The Simple Story

The woman had a daughter who was tormented by demons. She had obviously heard about Jesus, she had heard about the miracles and, apparently, she had heard how the Jews referred to Him when they asked for help. So she repeats what she believes to be the *"magic"* phrase, *"Jesus, O Son of David, help me"*. And Jesus completely ignores her.

The disciples interpreted this to mean He didn't care about her or her problem. So they want to get rid of her because *"she is bothering us with all her begging"*. I admit that I would have made the same faulty interpretation if I was one of the Twelve because Jesus' response to her would have had me deeply confused, too.

Now He turns and speaks to the woman telling her He was sent only to *"Israel, God's lost sheep, and not to the Gentiles"*. Of course, we know from other Bible stories, Jesus did help many Gentiles and in the Great Commission of Matthew 28 that He sends His disciples into the whole world. So why make the distinction between Jew and Gentiles now?

I believe the reason He does this is because this woman was not a Jew, yet she was claiming a Jewish relationship with Him by using the phrase, *"O Son of David"*. This is a very specific Old Testament phrase used to describe the Messiah who was promised to the Jews. It seems clear she had heard other Jews use this phrase and saw that Jesus responded to their cry for help.

So, instead of just asking for help as other Gentiles had done, she was being deceitful about her race and her relationship to Jesus. She was pretending to be something she was not. She was sincere, and desperate for help, to be sure; but deceitful, all the same.

Jesus now tells her He didn't come to help people *like her*. But instead of being offended and walking off in anger, she moves toward Him, draws near to Him and worships Him. Now Jesus seems to get downright mean and says, *"It isn't right to take food from the children and throw it to the dogs"*.

"Woman, you are a Gentile dog."

I can't even imagine how the scene unfolded or how I would have felt if I would have been there. This is way outside any frame of reference I have about the *"Compassionate Christ"*.

It would seem to me that the most important thing here would be the hurting daughter. Yet, it is clear that Jesus was trying to get to something far more *eternally* important in the heart of this woman; and in the hearts of His men who were standing there watching. I believe He is trying to get to something far more eternally important in our hearts, too.

An Amazing Response

After this insult, I would expect defensiveness, justification or angry indignation from this poor lady. But that is not her response. The King James Version is wonderfully simple here.

"And she said, **Truth, Lord***: yet the dogs eat of the crumbs which fall from their masters' table."*

(Matt. 15:27 KJV)

"That's the truth about me, Lord." That's it? That's her response to what I would have considered a real insult? Jesus had just called her a dog in front of all those other people. No wonder the disciples misunderstood.

I have been offended over a lot less than this. I confess I have broken off long time relationships over smaller things than this. I am not proud of it, but I know it's true.

And yet, this is her response – *"Truth, Lord. That's the truth about me. I have been pretending to have a relationship with You that I don't have. I have been pretending to be something I am not. I am not a Jew and I don't deserve anything from You. But as a dog, is there even a crumb You can give me?"*

Jesus responds with, *"Your faith is great"*, and heals her daughter.

The Faith To Stop Pretending

I confess I have unintentionally misrepresented this story in my preaching and teaching many times in the past. My only defense is that I just didn't understand *What God is really like* and *How He really feels about me.*

I thought this story was about having great faith for miracles, having great faith for mountains to be moved, having great faith so when troubles came I could just speak a word and my life would be easier. I no longer believe that is what Jesus was talking about, at all.

The woman obviously had some faith, some expectation in the miracle working power of Jesus or she would never have asked. But this is not the *"great faith"* Jesus referred to, at all.

It seems to be clear to me now that the faith Jesus is speaking about is the *faith to stop pretending* she was something she wasn't and still believe that God would help her because of who He is…He is good.

The Faith To Admit The Truth About Myself

This kind of faith is the willingness to admit the ugly truth about myself, my pretending, my deception; coupled with the confidence to believe that God already knows all of this about me…and He still wants to cure me.

Isaiah had the faith to stay in the *"great and terrible"* Presence of the most Holy God and believe He wouldn't kill him, but He would cure him.

Adam had enough faith to come back into the Presence of God and receive the cure. And it seems clear to me that he taught his children how to relate to God the same way; if they would make the same choice. Abel and Seth made the right choice, Cain did not.

Isaiah, Abel, Seth, Cain. I know which ones I want to imitate. *But I am just not sure how I can do it.*

Chapter Eighteen

A Whole Lot Of Jacob In Me

Genesis 32:24-32 tells a story that appears so strange that, without some solid frame of reference as to *What God is really like* and *How He really feels about me,* there is just no way to understand it. It's the story of Jacob wrestling with God.

The bizarre aspects of this encounter cause many to teach and preach some pretty far out things about how to *"Wrestle with God and get your blessing!"* More often than not, these interpretations come out more like this: *"How to twist God's arm into giving you what you want!"* I now believe this kind of thinking is just the opposite of what this story is really trying to teach us.

Scheming From the Womb

Here's the story. Jacob has been plotting and scheming his whole life about how to get the best for himself. I don't understand how it can happen, but before he even came out of the womb, he was trying to get ahead of his twin brother, pulling him back by the heel.

Because of this strange behavior his parents named him Jacob, which literally means *"to defraud, deceive, to supplant, i.e., to overthrow a person by tripping up his heels"*.

Jacob is an amazing study in contrasts. The meaning of his name and what his actions reveal about his heart become very important later in life. He schemes, he deceives and he pulls others back so he can get ahead. He learned how to spot the weaknesses of those around him and capitalize on them for his own benefit.

And yet, Jacob believed in the promises and blessings of God. Strange contrasts, and yet, I find the same things working in me to varying degrees. In the midst of all his selfishness and self-preservation, Jacob believed that the promises God made to his grandfather, Abraham, were true; and he wanted in on them.

His brother, Esau, didn't believe the promises. He placed no value in the stories that were passed down from his grandfather. The Bible says he *"despised"* them, meaning he demeaned them or de-valued them. He placed no importance on the promises of God made to his forefathers.

Jacob wanted the blessings of God but he didn't really want God. He wanted the promises but he didn't really want the *"Promisor"*. He didn't value a relationship with God and the few times he did encounter God, he was just happy to get away alive.

Jacob wanted to use the promises to get all the *"good things"* out of life. He wanted riches, safety and comfort. God wanted his heart. Jacob wanted his circumstances to change. God wanted to change Jacob. And fortunately for Jacob (*and for us*), God was determined to change the very core of who Jacob was.

Great Hope In A Strange Story

Part of what seems so strange about this story is that God, knowing everything about him, has chosen Jacob. The Bible is full of stories like this if we will just read them honestly. And I must admit this gives me great hope about myself. God saw something in Jacob's heart that his actions did not reveal and I desperately want Him to see that in me, too.

On the outside, Jacob looks totally self-absorbed. He appears to be willing to do most anything to get ahead, to prosper himself at the expense of others...and yet, God blesses him. He takes advantage of others...and yet, God blesses him. He lies to his own father and invokes the name of God to do it...and yet, God blesses him.

Virtually every "*hero of faith*" listed in Hebrews 11 has a history of fear, deception and sin, and yet, God saw something in their hearts with which He could work. And this, my friend, is our hope. Man sees on the outside, but God sees our hearts. And He is determined to keep working in us until He purifies us for His glory, ***if*** we will keep drawing near to Him for His cure.

It's easy for us to look back through the Scripture and see the plan of God for this "*supplanter*", this schemer, this self-promoter. But if we would have been there, seeing the heartache and humiliation being left in Jacob's wake, we would have wondered why God didn't fry him. Can't you just hear the thunder of judgment beginning to roll? That is, until we become honest enough to admit there is *a little bit of Jacob* in all of us. And for me, there is more than just a little bit. I think there must be a whole lot of Jacob in me.

Jacob Reaps What He Sows

The result of Jacob's selfish ambition was being forced to leave his family and home, everything that was dear to him, and hit the road in search of a new beginning. It had to be where people didn't know him; where people didn't know what he was really like. By God's design, he ended up with Uncle Laban. And the more we read, the stranger the story becomes.

It would do your heart good to read it for yourself in Genesis 27-32. As bizarre as this story seems, it tells us amazing things about *What God is really like* and *How He really feels about us.*

Esau realizes what Jacob has done and determines to kill him. Rebekah sends her deceiving son away to her brother. On the way, Jacob has an encounter with God, but instead of confessing his sin, he bargains with God for more blessing.

Jacob meets Laban's daughter, Rachel and agrees to work for seven years to earn the right to marry her. Laban deceives him on his wedding night and Jacob ends up with the wrong daughter. A little taste of his own medicine, I guess.

Jacob agrees to work another seven years for the right to finally marry the girl he wanted all along. And what follows is several years of these people deceiving each other. And yet, God is working in them every step of the way.

In the midst of God's blessing, they also reap from the anger and bitterness of their selfish actions. But God is moving Jacob toward an encounter that will bring him face to face with the hard truth about himself; and give him a chance at true transformation.

Esau Has Had Enough

Finally, after years of deception, scheming and cheating within this dysfunctional family, Jacob is on the run again with his wives, children and many possessions. A messenger comes with the news: after all these years, Esau has tracked him down and he's coming with an army to take revenge upon his brother.

What a perfect time to finally face the truth about himself and come clean before the Lord. Instead, Jacob makes the cowardly decision to offer up the lives of his own family in the hope that he might, once again, escape the well-deserved reaping that is about to come.

Jacob divides his family into two groups and sends them out to face the wrath of Esau. He is left alone and as night falls…God comes.

The abbreviated story is given to us in Genesis 32:24-32. In an effort to be consistent with so many other stories in the Scripture, please allow me the literary license to tell the story as it seems to me it must have occurred.

Jacob Faces God…And Confronts Himself

As night begins to fall, Jacob is left alone. Everything he has lied, schemed and deceived to get, is now gone and may never return. He has had many encounters with God, in a variety of situations, but he has never faced the truth about himself. This time, God comes in the form of a *"man"*.

We can't really understand how this happened any more than we can understand how God came to walk and talk with Adam in the garden. The fact that God would come to Jacob in the form of a man would be strange enough. But this story gets stranger still.

God, in the form of a man, begins to wrestle with Jacob. It seems this *"wrestling match"* continues through the night. I can't even begin to envision this. Whether this is an angel or an Old Testament appearance of the Christ, I don't know, no one knows, and I don't really care. But somehow, in some inexplicable way, God has condescended to rolling around in the dirt with this schemer, this deceiver...and He is after Jacob's heart.

For a while, Jacob seems to be winning, and as he does, he cries out, *"Bless me!"* Then the *"man"* seems to get the upper hand and Jacob is terrified that he won't get his blessing. Jacob thinks he is fighting for his life, but God is fighting to expose his heart.

Jacob declares, *"I won't let you go until you bless me"*, and the pushing and pulling in the dirt continues. At some point, the *"man"* touches Jacob's thigh and it pops out of joint. Incredibly painful, and yet Jacob doesn't give up. He won't admit the truth about himself, but he won't give up, either.

Then the *"man"* says a strange thing – *"What is your name?"* This is a rather odd thing for the all-knowing God to say in the midst of a wrestling match. Although, it's no more strange than the rest of the story.

Back To The Garden

My mind goes right back to the garden when God asks, "*Where are you?*" Of course, the Almighty knew exactly where they were hiding and why they were so afraid, ashamed and condemned. But He was inviting them to come back into His Presence and admit the truth about themselves so He could give them His cure. And we see the same thing happening here.

Of course, God knew Jacob's name. He knew him before he was born and He has been dealing with him for years. And God knew why Jacob was so afraid, ashamed and believing that judgment was coming in the form of his bloodthirsty brother. But God is after something in Jacob's heart.

So the wrestling match continues.

"I won't let you go until you bless me."

"What is your name?"

"I won't let you go until you bless me!"

"What is your name?"

What Is Your Name?

This is not the first time Jacob has been confronted with the question, "*What is your name?*" Years before when he was deceiving his father to get his brother's blessing, Isaac asks,

"What is your name?" Jacob refuses to admit the truth and says, *"I am your son, Esau"*. Isaac knows something isn't right. He reaches out and touches Jacob's hands and feels the hair, not knowing that Jacob had followed his mother's deceptive advice and covered has hands with animal hair to pretend to be Esau.

Then, Jacob's father says something that must have haunted Jacob for years. *"You feel like Esau but you sound like Jacob."*

And now God asks the same question; *"What is your name?"*

OK, I Admit The Truth

Finally, Jacob breaks down. Finally, he realizes that all of his fighting, scheming and manipulation isn't going to work. Finally, the deceiver admits the truth.

"Alright, I admit it. I am Jacob. I am the deceiver. I am the liar. I am the schemer. I am the one who has always acted in my own selfishness no matter who it hurt. I admit it. This is the truth about me. This is the ugly truth about who I am. I am the deceiver."

And a miracle happens! Right there in the dirt! After all this bizarre rolling around, fighting with a *"man"*, an *"angel of the Lord"*, Jacob finally admits the truth about himself.

And God immediately responds by saying –

"Not anymore! In this moment, I am changing you. You are no longer the deceiver. I am transforming you into Israel, a man who stands before Me as a prince!"

Wait a minute, what just happened?

Chapter Nineteen

Admit The Truth And Be Transformed

This story about Jacob wrestling with God has been the subject of countless sermons; many of them mine. And yet, I think I am just now starting to see how this admittedly bizarre story actually lines up with so many other Bible stories.

If we read them simply as they are written, we will find many Bible stories of people like Jacob. People who actually wrestled with themselves as God brought them to admit the truth about who and what they were, so He could transform them.

Jacob was a man who spent all his life cheating, deceiving and stealing whatever he wanted, no matter who it hurt. This was a man who had several miraculous encounters with God. But in every one, he bargained, he negotiated and he schemed for a way to save himself and come out ahead of everyone else.

God knew exactly what Jacob was doing and appeared to let him get away with it. But not this time. This time is the last time. This time Jacob is given only two choices; admit the truth about yourself and be changed, or be left completely on your own and reap the deadly consequences from what you have sown.

God was after Jacob's heart. And somewhere, under all the deception, was a man who really did want God and whatever God had for him. Because God knew the hearts of both Jacob and Esau before they were even born, He could say, *"I loved Jacob, but I rejected Esau."* (Rom. 9:13 NLT)

But for Jacob to get to the place where God could transform him, Jacob had to admit the truth about himself. Jacob had to admit that he had willingly chosen to become everything his name implied.

He was the deceiver, the schemer, the liar and he couldn't change himself. His only hope was a transforming encounter with God. The moment he admitted the truth about himself, God changed him. What a Brilliant Cure!

You Are The Guilty Man: *Yes I Am*

God described David as a *"man after My own heart"* while he was still young, even though He knew the sins David would commit. And when he committed the most horrendous sins, the prophet Nathan came to David with the word of the Lord and said *"You are the man."* (2 Sam. 12) David's response would determine the outcome; would he blame others or admit the truth about himself?

David's heart was exposed as he cried out, *"Yes, I am the guilty man. It's me. This is my sin, and mine, alone."* When David admitted the truth about himself, God's immediate response was, *"I have removed your sin from you and made you white as snow."*

We can hear David's heart in Ps. 51 as he says, *"Against You have I sinned...purify me...You desire truth in the inward parts..."*

"You desire truth in the inward parts." This is the pathway to God's cure for us. God is always using circumstances to bring us to a place where we will admit the truth about ourselves, truth in our *inward parts.*

This is exactly what Jacob finally came to admit, the truth in his inward parts. *"I am Jacob, I am a deceiver."* This is exactly what Isaiah confessed in God's most holy throne room; *"I am unclean."* This was the gentile woman's response to Jesus; *"Truth, Lord."*

Don't Lie To The Doctor

If I try to deceive the doctor about my symptoms, then I can't blame him if the medicine he prescribes doesn't work. If I deceive the doctor, I have no hope of getting help.

It doesn't matter what my motives are; embarrassment, fear or pride. I still can't get the help I need. I have to admit the truth about myself to get the medicine I need.

And if I understand this truth about human doctors who are just trying to help me because that is their job, how much more must I see this truth about the Heavenly Doctor who wants to help me because He truly loves me? I must admit the truth about myself to get the power of true, transforming grace.

Adam and Eve had to admit the truth about themselves, although like me, they didn't give up without a struggle. And, like me, the truth wasn't their first choice. There is always someone else I can blame.

The Blame Game

The human tendency to refuse to take responsibility for our failures, and blame others for our sin, comes to us naturally. It was passed down from our parents in the garden. But, if we allow it, this tendency will keep us from ever being truly changed, truly transformed.

When God asks, *"What have you done?"* Adam immediately blames Eve. He even blames God by saying, *"It was the woman that You gave me!"* When God speaks to Eve, she blames the serpent. When God speaks to the serpent he has no one to blame…there is no one left!

It seems clear that Adam and Eve learned an important lesson from this experience and were able to overcome this unwillingness to take the blame. Years later, we find that they taught their children how to take responsibility for their sin and make sacrifice to God. Cain and Abel clearly had a relationship with the God of their father.

When God speaks to Cain in Genesis 4, He makes it clear that Cain knew the right thing to do. And if he did what he had been taught, it would go well with him. He made the wrong choice.

It's Not My Fault

Jacob had the perfect people to blame for his weakness of character and failure in behavior; his parents.

"Isaac loved Esau…but Rebekah loved Jacob."

(Gen. 25:28)

I can only imagine what it must have been like growing up in a home where your father clearly favors your twin brother. And I can't imagine how I would feel once I was old enough to learn what my name actually meant; the name my parents used to brand me. And as Jacob grew, he certainly lived up to his name.

Perhaps because she knew Jacob was not loved by his father, Rebekah helped teach him how to deceive. She was actually his *"partner in crime"* in lying to his father and stealing the blessing that rightfully belonged to his brother.

But when God finally brought Jacob to the end of his own strength, he didn't blame anyone else. He could have, but he didn't. He chose to admit the truth about himself and he was forever transformed by the Presence of God.

David could have blamed Bathsheba for tempting him by bathing where he could see her. But when he admitted the truth about himself, the Presence of God changed him.

Zacchaeus could have blamed the Roman occupation of his homeland for why he became a tax collector and giving in to the temptation to take advantage of his people. But when he confessed the truth about himself, the Presence of Jesus transformed him.

Facing The Consequences

Each of these people had serious consequences to face because of their sins and God didn't take them all away. But you and I can face any consequence when we have been washed from fear, shame and condemnation. When we know we have been completely accepted by the Father, then we have true confidence with God; even when we have to reap difficult consequences.

The Holy Spirit can then empower us to live in the reality of Romans 8:28, *"And we know that all things work together for the good of them who love God..."* Our worst failures can be turned for our good, if, and only if, we admit the truth about ourselves and take the blame. After David admitted the truth about himself and faced the painful consequence of losing the baby born to Bathsheba, God gave them a new son; Solomon.

Changed By Truth In His Presence

Just encountering God, just experiencing His Presence, does not change us. Transformation depends on what we do in His Presence. Truth, transparency and taking the blame in His Presence is what allows the Holy Spirit to transform our lives.

Other people will always fall short of being all we think they should be. Our spouses, friends and strangers will mistreat us and give us plenty of excuses to act in ungodly ways and use the excuse that we are just protecting ourselves. But until we take the full blame for how we choose to react, we will never get free.

Isaiah had to admit he was unclean. If he would have walked away without that admission, or blamed his uncleanness on the unclean people around him, the angel could never have touched him and cleansed him.

If Jacob refused to admit the truth of his name and what that said about his character, he would have remained the schemer, faced Esau and been destroyed.

If Zacchaeus refused to acknowledge he was a cheat, he would have left that dinner the same as many of the Pharisees who ate with Jesus but remained lost in their deception.

But the problem with being deceived is...you usually don't know it when you are deceived. Or if you know, you don't want to admit it.

That's why God has given us the gift of the *two mirrors*.

God's Brilliant Cure

Chapter Twenty

God's Gift Of The Two Mirrors

Clearly, we have seen throughout the Bible that God's heart towards us is to cure our fear, shame and condemnation. And why would He do this? So we will learn to draw near to Him instead of drawing back. He wants us to draw near to Him, as we are, so He can change us and transform us into what He wants us to be; the likeness of His Son. That transformation begins as a down payment now. But it will be completed when we see Him face to face.

> *"Beloved, now we are children of God, and it has not appeared as yet what we will be. We know that when He appears, we will be like Him, because we will see Him just as He is."*
>
> (1 John 3:2)

Here is the down payment – *We are now the children of God.*

Here is the completion – *When He appears, we will be made like Him because we will see Him just as He is!*

The down payment in this life, the promise of transformation in this life, is accomplished as we understand, and take advantage, of God's *two mirrors*.

The Mirror Of The Word

James tells us that the *"mirror"* of the Word of God will show us what we are really like inside. But we must be willing to acknowledge the truth about ourselves if we are going to be changed.

> *"...he is like a man who looks at his natural face in a **mirror**; for once he has looked at himself and gone away, he has immediately forgotten what kind of person he was..."*
>
> (James 1:23-24)

We cannot ultimately change ourselves into the image of Jesus. But we can choose to agree with God when He shows us ourselves. And our agreement allows us access to the transforming power of the Spirit. The mirror of God's Word diagnoses what's wrong with us. Transformation depends on how we agree with the diagnosis.

I am learning to read the Word differently than I have ever read it before. I used to read the passages about all I should be and feel fear, shame and condemnation. Now I read it to see what God has done *for* me through the cross, what He wants to do *in* me by His Spirit, and what He will one day do *to* me when I see Him face to face.

We must learn to read the Word the same way we would listen to a doctor's diagnosis of our physical problem. Instead of feeling fear, shame or condemnation, we should listen to the doctor for the hope he can give us about a cure. This is the same way we should respond to the Heavenly Doctor's diagnosis of our condition as we look into the mirror of the Word.

The Mirror That Transforms Us

Paul speaks of another "*mirror*" that can transform us; and fundamentally change who and what we are.

> "*But we all, with unveiled face, beholding as in a **mirror** the glory of the Lord, are **being transformed** into the same image from glory to glory, just as from the Lord, the Spirit.*"

(2 Cor. 3:18)

This is the promise that if we will keep drawing near to God in prayer, praise and worship, we will keep being changed by His power. And what we are being changed into is the image of the very One we are worshipping. As we keep drawing near to God, He keeps changing us, more and more, into the image of His Son.

Paul uses an amazing word when he speaks of the transformation that occurs when we draw near to God. The Greek word he uses here is "*metamorphose*" and it is a very important word for us to understand.

Carnal Caterpillars Can Be Changed

Metamorphose is the same scientific word we use when describing what happens to a caterpillar as it *"transforms"* into a butterfly. This is what happens to a tadpole as it *"transforms"* into a frog. We can't explain this transformation, but we can experience it!

Metamorphose is the miracle of being fundamentally changed by a power far greater than ourselves. This is the promise of what the Holy Spirit will do in us every time we draw near to God *"in spirit and in truth"*. The Spirit wants to transform us from the inside out. This is the miracle of *metamorphose.*

Paul understood that this transformation, by the power of the Spirit working inside of us, was the true hope of Christ's resurrection. Because He was raised, we can be more than just forgiven; we can be changed. The message of the New Covenant is that the same Spirit who raised Christ from the dead will put His life inside of us. And He will change us from the inside out.

> *"If the same Spirit that raised Jesus from the dead lives in you, then He will put Christ's life into your mortal bodies."*
>
> (Rom.8:11, paraphrased)

This miracle of *metamorphose*, this miracle of transformation, renews our mind so we can see God as He really is, draw near to Him and be changed by the Spirit who lives in us.

> *"Therefore I urge you, brethren, by the mercies of God, to present your bodies a living and holy sacrifice,*

acceptable to God, which is your spiritual service of **worship**. *And do not be conformed to this world, but* **be transformed** *by the renewing of your mind..."*

(Rom. 12:1-2)

Again, Paul says that as we draw near to Him in worship, He transforms us. The metamorphosis we long for comes as we keep drawing near to Him. Every time I worship, I must expect God to lovingly reveal some truth about myself, be ready to admit it and let Him change me by the Spirit.

But This Does Not Happen Automatically

This is some of the greatest news I have ever heard. I can't change myself, but He can change me. And not only *can* He change me, *He really wants to change me.* Just like Adam, the Father keeps inviting me back into His Presence to work His cure in me.

But this miraculous transformation doesn't automatically happen. Sanctification doesn't just automatically occur. I have to keep presenting myself before the *"mirror"* of His Presence. This is my responsibility and no one can do this for me.

If I refuse to take the medicine the doctor gives me, I cannot blame him when I don't get well. If I choose to not take the medicine my Heavenly Doctor offers me, I have no one else to blame for not getting spiritually well but myself. I find God's medicine when I choose to draw near to Him in my weakness.

The Simple Choice – Draw Near or Draw Back

Adam and Eve had to come back into His Presence, as they were, to get His cure for their fear, shame and condemnation. He invited them in, but they had to act upon His invitation. They had to draw near. This was the medicine that would bring their cure.

Their first choice was to draw back in fear, but God gave them another opportunity to make a different choice. You and I always have the opportunity to make a different choice.

Because God has put away His anger, and He has put away our shame, we can come boldly before His throne and be changed by His Presence. But we must draw near, admit the truth about ourselves and interact with His Spirit in worship; and believe the Spirit will keep working to change us.

> "...let us **draw near** with confidence to the throne of grace, so that we may receive mercy and find grace to help in time of need."
>
> (Heb. 4:16)

> "...there is a bringing in of a better hope, through which we **draw near** to God."
>
> (Heb. 7:19)

> "...He is able also to save forever those who **draw near** to God through Him..."
>
> (Heb. 7:25)

*"...let us **draw near** with a sincere heart in full assurance of faith, having our hearts sprinkled clean from an evil conscience..."*

(Heb. 10:22)

This is what we must do; keep making the choice to either draw near or draw back. It doesn't get any more simple than this.

But if it's so simple, why would I ever draw back?

God's Brilliant Cure

Chapter Twenty One

What About Judgment And Wrath?

Fear, shame and condemnation are powerful motivators. But what they motivate us to do is never truly beneficial. These deep rooted feelings cause us to draw back rather than draw near to God for His cure. Fear, shame and condemnation motivated Adam and Eve to hide from the only One who loved them and could cure them.

Fear, shame and condemnation produce overwhelming feelings of hopelessness and helplessness that steal confidence and drive people to draw back and give up. More suicides come from this sense of hopelessness than any other source. But the Good News is supposed to be the true source of real hope; "*the hope of the nations*".

And yet, most of us have unwittingly bought into the lie that God motivates us to obey Him through fear of punishment or the shame of not being as perfect as we should be. We are frequently taught that we are supposed to fear God's punishment for our lack of perfection and be ashamed of our weakness because He must surely be angry and ashamed of us.

However, a simple and honest reading of the scripture should drive us to ask ourselves the same question God asked Adam and Eve; *"Who told you that?"*

Who told me that...I should be afraid of the Father?

Who told me that...I should be ashamed in His Presence?

Who told me that...He would reject me because of my human weakness?

Who told me that...adverse circumstances come from God's judgment for my lack of Christ-likeness?

Who told me that???

Wait a minute. If it is true that God does not motivate us by fear and shame, then what are we going to do with all those verses that seem to tell us we must *"Fear the great and terrible God"*?

Context, Context, Context

Again, we have to begin where God begins. We must *start at the right starting point* if we are going to relate to Him correctly. And we must learn to read the Bible in context, comparing scripture with scripture, if we are going to understand what God is saying to us.

In Exodus 34, God certainly spoke about fearful judgment, but only for those who do not choose His compassion, mercy and forgiveness.

Heb 10:31 tells us *"It is a terrifying thing to fall into the hands of the living God."* But we must read the whole chapter.

The writer is warning us, and more specifically, warning Jewish (Hebrew) Christians, that *"if we go on sinning after we have received the knowledge of the truth"* by trusting in the Old Way of priest, sacrifice, shadow and human effort, then we have *"trampled under foot the Son of God...regarded as unclean the blood of the covenant...and have insulted the Spirit of grace."*

Though I once trusted in some of those now obsolete things, that is no longer me and, if you have placed your trust in God's unfailing love through the sacrifice of Jesus Christ, it's not you, either! We can now live in, and actually enjoy, the true meaning of the biblical word, *"fear"*.

Tormenting Fear or Deep, Holy Reverence

The Hebrew word translated *"fear"* throughout the Old Testament is used to describe **both** the *terrifying fear of an angry judge* and the *deep reverence given to a father*. So how do we know what the word *"fear"* means? It all depends on the context in which it is used.

When describing Himself in Exodus 34, God gives us the choice of how we want to relate to Him based on the evidence He gives us about Himself. We can choose to relate to Him as our Father, full of mercy and compassion, always willing to forgive every manner of sin, iniquity and transgression.

Or, we can refuse His free gift of love and choose to relate to Him as the Righteous Judge. He gives us that choice but He keeps revealing Himself to us as He really is so we can make the right choice...if we choose to believe what He says.

The Beginning Of Wisdom

When I first began to seriously question if my understanding of what God wanted from me was correct, I went to Proverbs 9:10, *"The fear of the Lord is the beginning of wisdom."* The connection of fear and wisdom in passages like this is very important.

I taught my children to be afraid of what fire can do if used incorrectly. I wanted them to gain wisdom about fire's destructive power if it is used inappropriately. But I never wanted them to break out in a terrifying sweat every time someone turned on the stove or lit a candle. This kind of fearful respect for the destructive power of fire does not lead to a terrifying fear of candles but it is *the beginning of wisdom* in how to correctly relate to fire.

Certainly, the Bible portrays God as the Almighty, All Powerful God; and there is a fearful expectation of judgment awaiting any who reject His absolute authority. If we choose to ignore His ownership over everything, we face a terrifying end, separated from Him forever. That is our choice, not His.

But when we start where He wants us to start in our understanding of Him, we revere Him as the Almighty, All Powerful *Father* who has gone to great lengths to demonstrate His love and care for us. And we find rest in His love.

*"But God **demonstrates His own love toward us**, in that while we were yet sinners, Christ died for us. **Much more then**, having now been justified by His blood, we shall be **saved from the wrath** of God through Him. For if while we were enemies we were reconciled to God through the death of His Son, **much more**, having been reconciled, we shall be saved by His life."*

(Rom. 5:8-11)

Paul clearly tells us we can either respond to the demonstration of God's love through the cross and be saved from the wrath of God, both now and at the final judgment; or we can choose to remain His enemy.

That is our choice, not His. His choice was to send His Son to make it perfectly clear to all creation how He really feels about us.

I have made my choice to respond to the demonstration of His love for me. But in order for me to live free of fear, shame and condemnation, I must **know** and **believe** what He says about His judgment and wrath. If I don't **know** and **believe** the truth, the accuser will continually steal my confidence towards God.

What Happened To Judgment And Wrath?

For me to see *What God is really like* and *How He really feels about me*, I have to have my mind and understanding renewed; regularly renewed. To be renewed in my thinking, I have to see, and believe, what the Word of God actually says.

Not what I thought it said, not what I have been told it says, but what the Word simply says.

Jesus made it clear that by responding to God's love and receiving His free gift, we are freed from God's judgment.

> *"God so loved the world...He gave His only Son...God did not send the Son into the world to judge the world...he who believes in Him **is not judged**."*
>
> (John 3:16-18)

Jesus told us what was going to happen to God's righteous judgment and wrath, but this amazing truth has gotten *"lost in translation"* and faulty interpretation. And this one mistaken belief has caused more fear, shame and condemnation that any single other tool the enemy has in his arsenal. Millions of believers around the world have lived without the confidence they are entitled to because of this one faulty interpretation.

This is not an accusation against others who may teach differently. I made this same mistake for years and I lived with the fearful torment this erroneous belief causes.

But I am on a journey to get free...and stay free! *And here's how...*

Chapter Twenty Two

Why Was He *"Lifted Up"*?

When I became a Christian as a young hippie in 1967, I was told by some sincere people that the King James Version was the only true Bible. Many of the verses I memorized in those early days I still remember in the language of the KJV.

I am going to give you a very well known passage from the gospel of John. I have quoted this passage hundreds of times without ever realizing I completely misunderstood the truth it contains.

> *"Now is the judgment of this world: now shall the prince of this world be cast out. And I, if I be lifted up from the earth, will draw all (men) unto me."*
>
> (John 12:31-32 KJV)

For years I have believed this passage had a two-fold meaning. One, Jesus would be lifted up on the cross and that *"lifting up"* would draw all men to Him. Two, if we lift Him up by declaring His name in preaching and worship, then all men would be drawn to Him. But these interpretations immediately present some serious problems.

Jesus was lifted up on the cross and His name has been lifted up for centuries, but all men have not been drawn to Him. Some have, but not nearly all. Something is wrong with the generally accepted interpretations of this passage. Now I see there is a much bigger problem here because this is not actually what Jesus said, at all.

The King James Version of the Bible, completed in 1611, was the first major effort to translate the scripture into English and it has been rightly revered ever since. Due to the difficulty of translating from an ancient language into seventeenth century English, the translators added certain words to make the text clearer.

They italicized the added words so the reader would know these words were not in the original texts or available manuscripts. And in most places the additional words help clarify the meaning. But in this case we have a serious problem with the phrase, *"if I be lifted up from the earth, will draw all **men** unto me."*

In the KJV, the word *"men"* is in italics, meaning it was added by the translators. The word *"men"* is not in any manuscript. If we leave the word *"men"* out, now the passage actually reads:

*"...I, if I be lifted up from the earth, will draw **all** unto me."*

"*Draw **all** unto me*"...draw all what? He clearly says He will draw **all** of something to Himself, but **all** of what? Since Jesus did not use the word "*men*", then the question becomes, "*What did He actually draw to Himself?*"

What Did Jesus Really Say?

The subject of the larger passage is ***judgment***. "*Now is the **judgment** of this world.*" When we read it in context, the passage actually says,

> "*Now is the **judgment** of this world: now shall the prince of this world be cast out. And I, if I be lifted up from the earth, will draw all (**judgment**) unto me.*"
>
> (John 12:31-32)

It certainly appears Jesus is saying that the judgment of the whole world would be placed upon Him when He was lifted up on the cross. But this issue of God's judgment is so important we must not impose our own ideas or opinions here. Our standard for truth must be what the Word of God clearly and simply says.

This is eternally important so we must be right in what we believe. If we don't understand what they understood, we cannot believe what they believed. If we don't believe what they believed, we will never have the confidence they had.

But how can we know what Jesus actually said and what He actually meant? How can we find the *simple* meaning of His words? We can find it by comparing a similar statement

Jesus made to Nicodemus and understanding the plain, simple context.

As The Serpent Was Lifted Up

We have already seen in John 3:18 that Jesus promised anyone who believes in Him "*is not judged*". If we back up to verse 16 we find the reason for this is that "*God loves the world so much that He gave His Son*". But if we back up to verses 14-15, we find the clear declaration that freedom from judgment comes because...

> "*As Moses lifted up the serpent in the wilderness, even so must the Son of Man be lifted up; so that whoever believes in Him will have eternal life.*"
>
> (John 3:14-15)

In His conversation with Nicodemus, an expert in the Old Testament, Jesus makes a direct comparison to Him being lifted up on the cross and God instructing Moses to make a bronze serpent and lift it up on a standard or a stake.

The people had sinned by continually accusing God, and Moses, of not caring for them; even though God had repeatedly demonstrated His love through miraculous acts. Judgment came in the form of serpents because the people chose to remain in hardhearted unbelief. You can read the full account in Numbers 21.

When Jesus made this direct comparison to Nicodemus, the sincere Pharisee could not have fully understood about the coming cross. But he did understand about God taking His judgment and placing it on the serpent; and that the people who looked on it in faith were released from God's judgment.

> *"And Moses made a bronze serpent and set it on the standard; and it came about, that if a serpent bit any man, when he looked to the bronze serpent, he lived."*
>
> (Num. 21:5)

Isn't this exactly what happened on the cross? The ***judgment*** of the whole world was placed upon Jesus.

> *"...He Himself is the propitiation for our sins; and not for ours only, but also for those of the **whole world**."*
>
> (1 John 2:2)

Just as the judgment against Israel was placed upon the serpent and lifted up above the people, Jesus said the judgment of the whole world would be placed upon Him as He was lifted up on the cross. When we read what Jesus said to Nicodemus, we see a powerful metaphor of what would happen, both to judgment, and to the power of the prince of this world.

> *"Now is the judgment of this world: now shall the prince of this world be cast out."*
>
> (John 12:31)

> *"If I am lifted up, I will draw it all to me."*
>
> (John 12:32)

"...when he looked to the bronze serpent, he lived."

(Numbers 21:5)

This metaphor is completely consistent with the rest of the Word. Listen to the most powerful description of the crucifixion in the whole Bible and see the judgment that Jesus willingly drew to Himself!

"...stricken by God, smitten by him, and afflicted;

...pierced for our transgressions;

...crushed for our iniquities;

...the punishment that brought us peace was upon him;

...the LORD has laid on him the iniquity of us all;

...it was the LORD's will to crush him, cause him to suffer;

...the LORD makes his life a guilt offering;

...he will bear their iniquities;

...he bore the sin of many..."

(Isa. 53:4-6 NIV)

Jesus knew what lay before Him. He willingly came into the world for this purpose. The Father and the Son agreed on a **Brilliant Plan** that would satisfy justice and cause mercy to triumph over judgment…for us! He took it all upon Himself!

So What Must I Do To Live Free?

The picture is simple, clear and complete. All that remains for me to do is what I am responsible to do: believe that God tells the truth. I must believe He tells the truth about *What He is really like* and *How He really feels about me*.

For this to work in our lives, we must make the same choice Israel had to make. They had to put aside their unbelief and choose to agree with God. They had to agree that they were guilty and that God, in His great love, had their cure.

We must look upon His sacrifice for us, confess the truth about ourselves and believe that God is telling the truth when He says He has our cure. We must believe that in His great love for us, He truly wants to set us free from fear, shame and condemnation. We must believe this was His idea, out of His great love, for our benefit.

I want to believe this amazing Good News, I really do. But it seems that every time something goes wrong, every time trouble comes, every time my prayers don't get answered the way I want them to, I fall back into the same old fearful thinking. My mind seems to have a *mind of its own*.

Clearly, I need a good *"brain-washing"*.

Chapter Twenty Three

Rainbows and Brain Washings

The literal meaning of the word **condemnation** is *"a fearful expectation of judgment or punishment"*. It is the all too common feeling that says, *"If I don't live up to the perfect image of Christ then the Father will be angry with me, judge me and, very possibly, punish me."*

Perhaps He won't hear my prayer and help me. Or, I will miss my destiny and never find the *"perfect will of God"*. Or, at the very least, He will step back and let the devil take a shot at me...or my family...or my finances...or my health. And that kind of thinking certainly produces *"a fearful expectation of judgment or punishment"*; it produces condemnation.

These tormenting thoughts come from the *"accuser"* and we all share in the battle. That's why we must learn to live in a clear understanding of the importance of *"Rainbows and Brain Washings"*.

If all judgment was placed upon Jesus when He was on the cross, then you and I can live free from any and all expectation of judgment or punishment. Then we can live free from constantly trying to interpret every bad circumstance to see if it's from God or the devil. Or trying to discern if trouble came because we somehow missed the *"perfect will of God"*. We really can live free from this condemnation; not just in heaven, but here and now.

Until condemnation is removed we will never be able to draw near to God and receive His cure when we fall short. And it is when we fail and fall short that we need His cure the most.

Until our hearts and minds are washed from old ways of thinking, we are doomed to fall into the same old traps. We desperately need regular *"brain washings"* so we can think differently than we have in the past; so we can put our faith in something very different than we have in the past.

Fear of Rain and The Assurance of Rainbows

From Isaiah 54, we have seen that God made us an absolute promise. He felt so strongly about this promise, He swore! And when God swears, it's a big deal to Him. Just as He swore a promise to Noah, He has sworn a promise to us.

> *"For this is like the days of Noah to Me, when I swore that the waters of Noah would not flood the earth again; so **I have sworn** that **I will not be angry with you** nor will I rebuke you."*

(Is. 54:9)

After the horrific flood Noah and his family went through, God understood what would happen to their hearts and minds every time it started to rain again. The same old fears of judgment and the terror of a coming wrath would rise up in them, again and again. How could they help it after what they had experienced?

But God wanted them to be free of those torments. He wanted them to be able to enjoy the process of rain because, what first came as judgment and punishment, would now come to produce growth. So God gave them a sign to reassure their hearts and renew their minds every time it began to rain.

"I set My bow in the cloud...It shall come about, when I bring a cloud over the earth, that the bow will be seen in the cloud, and I will remember My covenant...And God said to Noah, This is the sign of the covenant which I have established between Me and all flesh that is on the earth."

(Gen. 9:13-17)

Every time it started to rain and the old fear began to rise, Noah could look to the sky, see the rainbow, and be washed from his fear. For the rest of their lives the rainbow would reassure them that God keeps His word of promise. They could have a good *brain washing* every time they looked to the sky and saw God's covenant sign. But they had to look to the sky and choose to believe that God told them the truth when He made that promise.

Reminding, Reassuring and Renewing

God doesn't ever forget, but people do. The biblical terminology of God *"remembering"* is a way to communicate to us on our human level. The rainbow wasn't really a reminder for God; it was a reminder for Noah.

Every time Noah saw the rainbow he was reminded that God was thinking about him and that He would keep His covenant promise. And Noah's heart and mind were washed from fear again.

The people of God were supposed to take the sign of the rainbow as a constant reminder of His goodness to them. Ezekiel certainly did. His mind was washed with the same reassurance when God revealed His glory to him.

> "**As the appearance of the rainbow** in the clouds on a rainy day, **so was the appearance** of the surrounding radiance. Such was the appearance of the likeness of the glory of the LORD."
>
> (Ezk. 1:28)

The people of God had once again turned from Him and Ezekiel had a very serious prophetic message for them. But instead of being terrified by the appearance of God's glory, Ezekiel was reassured of God's goodness for him. His mind was washed from fear, shame and condemnation.

God knows we must be constantly washed and regularly reminded. He understands our weakness and He knows the tactics of the "*accuser*". (Rev. 12:10) So, in the New Covenant, He has given us the ultimate sign to wash our minds and reassure our hearts. He has given us an eternal sign that can make us immovable and unshakable; no matter how much trouble may come.

Our Sign In The Sky

Hebrews 8:6 tells us that we have a *better covenant* made on *better promises*! And we have been given a sign we can look to every time trials, tribulations and unanswered questions cause that old fear to start rising up again. Our sign in the sky is the cross of Christ. Every time we look to the cross, it is intended to be a constant reminder of all that was accomplished there…for us.

> *"…having canceled out the certificate of debt consisting of decrees against us, which was hostile to us; and He has taken it out of the way,* **having nailed it to the cross.***"*
>
> (Col. 2:14)
>
> *"…having made peace through the blood of* **His cross.***"*
>
> (Col. 1:20)
>
> *"He, Himself, bore our sins in His body* **on the cross***…"*
>
> (1 Peter 2:24)

The apostolic writers made it clear that our covenant sign is the cross. The cross is what they remembered in order to keep washing their hearts and minds from the fear and torment of condemnation. The cross doesn't remind God of what He has done; it reminds us of what He has done for us. And that reminder washes our minds, our hearts and our emotions.

Once And For All!

Each time the apostolic writers looked to the cross, they were powerfully reminded that this sacrifice was not just a historical fact in the past, but an eternal fact, once and for all. The cross was their constant reminder that...

– The payment for all sin was made...*once and for all.*

– Our full acceptance into God's unearned favor was done...*once and for all.*

– Our adoption as His children was accomplished...*once and for all.*

– And our freedom from fear, shame and condemnation was purchased...*once and for all!*

*"For Christ also died for sins **once for all**, the just for the unjust, so that He might bring us to God..."*

(1 Peter 3:18)

*"For the death that He died, He died to sin **once for all**."*

(Rom. 6:10)

*"...this He did **once for all** when He offered up Himself."*

(Heb. 7:27)

*"...through His own blood, He entered the holy place **once for all.**"*

(Heb. 9:12)

*"By this will we have been sanctified through the offering of the body of Jesus Christ **once for all.**"*

(Heb. 10:10)

Healthy Brain Washings By The Spirit

These are the *"once and for all"* truths we must wash our minds and reassure our hearts with over and over again. As believers, adopted together into the family of God, we can vigorously debate things like *"eternal security"* or *"progressive sanctification"* and not allow our differing views to divide us. But there must be no doubt about our full acceptance which was purchased by Jesus' sacrifice on the cross...*once and for all!*

*"Because of Christ and our faith in him, **we can now come fearlessly into God's presence, assured of his glad welcome.**"*

(Eph. 3:12-13)

Because of the cross, we have the complete assurance of God's full acceptance of us. Now we can get the benefit of the Holy Spirit regularly washing our hearts and minds by filling our lives with this amazing truth.

*"Therefore, brethren, since we have confidence to enter the holy place by the blood of Jesus...and since we have a great priest over the house of God, **let us***

> *draw near with a sincere heart in full assurance of faith,* **having our hearts sprinkled clean from an evil conscience and our bodies washed with pure water.**"
>
> (Heb. 10:21-22)

Based on what Jesus has done for us, we can draw near to God in full assurance of faith. When we draw near to Him we can expect the Holy Spirit to wash our conscience clean; not based on what we have done, but based on what Jesus has done for us.

The writer of Hebrews makes it very clear what the price of confident entry is when he says, "...*we have confidence to enter the holy place* ***by the blood of Jesus.***" If we try to draw near based on our own merit then our conscience will condemn us, because we are never good enough. But the blood of Jesus ***IS*** good enough to purchase our entry into the holy place with God.

How Good Do You Have To Be?

How good is good enough, anyway? We will never be good enough by our own effort for the measure of Christ's perfectness. Being good in our own ability is not even the goal of this life. The goal is to rest in His merit, grow in the power and image of His life within us...and to be at peace with the knowledge that we will never be perfect here; but we will be *made perfect* there.

I want to continually live in this New Covenant peace and rest where I am free from fear, shame and condemnation. And

I am beginning to see this can only happen to the degree that I experience regular *"brain washings"* by the Spirit of Truth. But these *"brain washings"* can only be effective as I learn to enter in and enjoy **fellowship** with the Almighty God.

Fellowship? When I think of fellowship halls and fellowship dinners, I begin to suspect I don't define the word *"fellowship"* the same way the early believers defined it. They seem to have considered fellowshipping God as the prime reason Jesus came to the earth. It seems to have been extremely important to them; far more important than it has been to me.

Apparently, I don't understand what true fellowship actually means. *And here I go again; having to redefine something I thought I already knew.*

Chapter Twenty Four

The Transforming Power Of Fellowshipping God

I said near the beginning of this book that one of the most important things for us to learn from the story of Adam and Eve is that God wanted them to live in *fellowship* with Him. Adam and Eve were so important to God that He wanted to spend time with them; apparently, everyday. Grab onto this very important truth. God, the Almighty, wanted to spend time fellowshipping what began essentially as two walking, talking piles of dirt!

What He made, He loved; deeply loved. Knowing what they were going to do, He loved them; deeply. After knowing they sinned, He wanted to be with them; and He wanted them to be with Him. This demonstrates the importance of fellowship.

Knowing us, and our weaknesses, He wants us to be with Him and He wants to be with us. We have a High Priest who understands our weaknesses (Heb. 4:15), and He longs to interact with us deeply and intimately, in our weaknesses. He wants to listen to us as we pour out our hearts to Him. And He wants us to listen to Him as He pours out His heart to us…knowing our weaknesses.

Adam and Eve's sin caused them to need a cure, but their sin didn't change the fact that God wanted to fellowship with them. In fact, they could only get His cure if they came back into His presence; they had to come back into fellowship with Him. They had to stop drawing back and once again draw near to get the medicine He was offering. Fellowship is all about learning to draw near when we do well or when we fail.

When they stopped hiding behind that tree and once again drew near to Him, He fixed their problem through sacrifice. That sacrifice, and every sacrifice that followed throughout the Old Testament, was a shadow of the permanent cure He was going to bring through the sacrifice of Jesus on the cross.

Hope For Earthen Vessels

You and I can now live in the permanent cure He provided, once and for all, by our faith in the finished work of the cross and the present work of the Spirit in us. Even though we are still *"earthen vessels"*, God wants to keep putting the glory of His presence within us. Paul understood this essential truth when he said *"...we have this treasure in **earthen vessels**, so that the surpassing greatness of the power will be of God and not from ourselves."* (2 Cor. 4:7) In the previous verses he tells us that this *"treasure"* is the *"light of the glory of God shining into us through the knowledge Christ".*

The very fact that God wants to keep pouring His presence into us while we are still *"earthen vessels"* shows how He feels about us. And He does this *SO THAT* all may see that it's His work, out of His goodness. This is what gives hope to others who suffer from fear, shame and condemnation; just as we do.

This treasure of the glory of God shining into our lives cannot be earned by our good behavior, nor can we qualify for it by our personal sacrifice. But we can enjoy it by putting our faith in what He has said about us and what He has done for us.

When we choose to believe He is telling the truth concerning how He really feels about us in our *"earthiness"*, the Holy Spirit responds by drawing us into fellowship with Him. It is in fellowshipping God that our mind is renewed, our conscience is washed clean and our heart is filled with the love of the Father.

Koinonia – Intimate Interaction With God

The greek word translated *"fellowship"* is <u>koinonia</u>. Literally translated, koinonia means *"interaction, intercourse or communion"*. It is used to describe the deepest life-giving interaction between God and a person; or between a person and another person. The New Testament writers used the word *koinonia* very sparingly, and never in a casual way. It was a deeply meaningful word to those early believers.

Remember, they didn't have the New Testament. The gentile believers didn't even have the Old Testament. They didn't have books, CDs, or DVDs. All they had was fellowship with God and fellowship with each other as the Body of Christ.

In fact, John boldly declares that the entire reason Jesus came into the world was to bring us into *koinonia, fellowship, intimate, life-giving interaction* with God; and intimate, life-giving interaction with each other as His family on the earth.

> *"What was from the beginning, what we have heard, what we have seen with our eyes, what we have looked at and touched with our hands, concerning the Word of Life...what we have seen and heard we proclaim to you also,* **so that you too may have fellowship with us; and indeed our fellowship is with the Father, and with His Son, Jesus Christ."**
>
> (1 John 1:1-3)

Think of the importance of this statement.

> *The Word of Life (Jesus) came into the world, we saw it and touched it, and we have declared it to you SO THAT...we can have koinonia with each other because we enter into koinonia with the Father and the Son.*

Jesus came into the world so we could have true fellowship with God. And now that we are part of the family of God, we can have true fellowship with each other. Paul uses this same image to help us understand that the transforming power of New Covenant life depends on how we learn to understand and participate fully, and frequently, in fellowshipping God.

> *"God is faithful, through whom you were* **called into fellowship** *(koinonia) with His Son, Jesus Christ our Lord."*
>
> (1 Cor. 1:9)

We are not called to just believe in the Son, but we have been called to come into fellowship with Him. We are called to engage in true, transforming interaction with Him. This is how we are washed, renewed and transformed.

> *"The **grace** of the Lord Jesus Christ, and the **love** of God, and **the fellowship of the Holy Spirit**, be with you all."*
>
> (2 Cor. 13:14)

Let me paraphrase Paul's desire for them, and us, based on the literal meaning of these important words.

> *"May the unearned power of Christ's life within you (grace)...and the assurance of the unconditional and unwavering love of God... and the intimate, internal interaction of the Holy Spirit...be working in all of you."*
>
> (2 Cor. 13:14, paraphrased)

This is the New Covenant life we have been called to experience. This is what cures us from our fear, shame and condemnation. This is our rightful inheritance through Jesus Christ. Anything less than this amazing life of freedom is a cheap imitation of the true New Covenant.

The New Covenant is not based on a list of rules that humans must try hard to keep in order to appease an angry God. The New Covenant is based on intimate interaction with the Father and the Son through the work of the Spirit who lives in every believer. The Old Covenant was based on external rules to be kept by human effort. But the New Covenant is based on internal interaction with Christ who lives in us by His Spirit. And this fellowship, this intimate interaction, produces life. It produces *His* life within us!

Christ's Life Is Being "*Conceived*" Inside Us

As uncomfortable as it may feel in our sanitized, watered down, western thinking, the word *koinonia* also means *"intercourse";* and it has the clear implication of *conception.* It really does mean that God wants to keep *impregnating* us with His divine life.

This contains a powerful lesson for us as we seek to be progressively changed by the power of the Spirit. As we learn to fellowship Him, the Holy Spirit keeps filling us with His life, conceiving and forming His image within us. He keeps *impregnating* us with His life!

> *"...if the Spirit of Him who raised Jesus from the dead dwells in you, He who raised Christ Jesus from the dead will also **give life to your mortal bodies** through His Spirit who dwells in you."*
>
> (Rom. 8:11)

As we learn to fellowship God through the Spirit, He will keep putting His life into our mortal bodies. He does this *"through the Spirit who dwells in you".* As we learn to intimately interact with the Holy Spirit, we are being changed by His life, which is being formed within us.

Christ's Life Is Being "Formed" Inside Us

Paul gave a strong rebuke to the believers in Galatia when they began returning to the old way of thinking that they could somehow produce the life of God by human effort; by trying hard to keep all the rules by their own work. Though they started their life in Christ, by putting their faith in His love, His power, and His work inside of them, they were now trying to change themselves by human effort...by *"trying harder to be better"*.

> *"Have you lost your senses? After starting your Christian lives in the Spirit, why are you now trying to become perfect by your own human effort?"*
>
> (Gal. 3:3) NLT

Then he makes reference to the transforming work of the Holy Spirit as He keeps changing us from the inside out. But he uses a very mysterious phrase to describe this mysterious process of the life of Christ growing within us.

> *"My children, with whom I am in labor until Christ is **formed in you again**..."*
>
> (Gal. 4:19)

"...until Christ is formed in you again..."?!

These can seem like very strange words unless we understand the power of fellowship and how the Spirit transforms us from the inside out as we intimately interact with Him. This is the promise of the New Covenant: *the life of Christ will grow inside of us as we learn to fellowship Him by the Spirit. We are transformed by His working in and through us.*

Paul was not referring to their salvation but to their sanctification, their growth in grace, their internal transformation as the Spirit continued to mold them into His image. I can't explain this. Neither could Paul, so he called it a mystery. It's a divine process that is beyond human understanding. Though I can't explain it, I am experiencing it.

I am learning what this mysterious process of fellowshipping God can produce. I am learning that the very transformation my heart hungers for can only come through this process of fellowship; by intimately interacting with Him by His Spirit.

I am also learning that this transforming fellowship is not automatic. It requires my deliberate choice and my intentional cooperation.

Just as God's cure for Adam and Eve required that they choose to stop hiding behind that tree and intentionally draw near to Him, this on-going transformation requires that you and I choose to stop allowing fear, shame and condemnation to make us draw back. We must choose to believe the truth of what He says about His love for us and keep drawing near to Him in fellowship.

But if this transforming power of fellowshipping God requires my deliberate action…*what must I choose to do?*

Chapter Twenty Five

The Deliberate Choices – Feed, Focus and Faith

The deliberate process of fellowship depends on the choices we make. Though we cannot ultimately transform ourselves by human effort, we have been given the power to choose what we *feed* on, *focus* on, and put our *faith* in.

What we feed on will determine how we grow. What we focus on, reflects back upon us. And these two things will transform us when we put our faith in them. But the choice is always ours.

Adam and Eve had the power to choose to draw near to God, after their sin, and receive His cure. Isaiah had the power to choose to stay in God's presence and be cleansed, even though he was afraid because of his uncleanness. Jacob had the power to choose to admit the truth about himself and be changed; even though he was exhausted, afraid and in pain.

The transforming power of actively fellowshipping God by the Spirit is something we can, and must, deliberately choose. Transforming fellowship involves what we choose to eat (*feed*), how we choose to frame our worship (*focus*), and what we choose to put our confidence in (*faith*).

Feed / Focus / Faith

We learn to fellowship God by choosing to *feed* ourselves on what the Word simply, plainly, and truthfully tells us.

We frame our *focus* by constantly choosing to intimately interact with His Spirit and framing our worship on the truth of His word, and not our fearful feelings. We must deliberately choose to behold the beauty of His Holiness instead of being afraid of it, and magnify the majesty of *what He is really like* and *how He really feels about us*.

We place our *faith* in Him, and His work in us, when we keep choosing to believe He tells the truth about *what He is really like* and *how He really feels about us*.

Feed On The True Word

The written word, the Bible, is referred to as both milk and meat; or solid food. We must learn to eat it correctly.

> *"...like newborn babies, long for the pure milk of the word, so that by it you may grow in respect to salvation."*
>
> (1 Peter 2:2)

> *"I gave you milk to drink, not solid food; for you were not yet able to receive it."*
>
> (1 Cor. 3:2)

Both milk and meat (solid food) are important for our growth. For us to fellowship God, we must feed on what He has already said; the written word of God. It is certainly true that God wants to speak to us regularly by His Spirit, now, in our fellowship with Him.

But for us to understand what He is saying to us now by His Spirit, we must understand the truth of what He has already said in His written word.

Throughout this book we have looked at dozens of bible passages. Hopefully, we have discovered that we have often misunderstood what the Word is saying. My strong suggestion is that we learn to look at the Word with two important thoughts in mind – *simplicity and context*.

The Simplicity Of The Word

For many years I attempted to be "*deep*" in my teaching. I enjoyed having people come up to me after a Sunday service and say, *"Oh, Pastor, that message was so deep!"* Until one day my wife lovingly said to me, *"Honey, I think you may not understand what they mean when they say 'deep'. They may be saying that they really didn't have any idea what you were talking about, so they assumed you were "so deep".*"

That's when it dawned on me that I had been trying to be so deep, and apparently confusing, that my own wife didn't understand what I was talking about. Now I am looking for truth that is simple and plain; and understood by its context.

Paul was very concerned that the early believers would be led astray by complicated teachings that put the emphasis on them and their effort, instead of the simplicity of interacting with the Spirit of Christ who lived within them.

Old Covenant Law always puts the emphasis on you and what you must do…and it's very complicated. Just read through the book of Leviticus and you will either get a headache or it will cure your insomnia. But New Covenant truth always puts the emphasis on Christ and what He wants to do inside of you; and it's simple.

Listen to Paul's deep concern for the early believers –

*"But I am afraid that, as the serpent deceived Eve by his craftiness, your minds will be led astray from the **simplicity** and **purity of devotion** to Christ."*

(2 Cor. 11:3)

Eve was led astray by the promise that there was something she could do that could make her wise, apart from drawing near to God. She ate the fruit because it was *"desirable to make one wise"* by her human effort, apart from fellowshipping God. (Gen. 3:6) But God had created them so that everything they needed to know would come to them from Him; by simply interacting *(fellowshipping)* with Him.

I now have an obsession to be simple; simple and plain. To understand what the Word actually means, I look for the simple answer first. I look for the plain meaning of words.

Don't take anything I have said in this book, or any other book, and believe it just because I said it. Read it for yourself and see if the simple, plain meaning comes through. Look for the *"main and plain"* truths, not the supposedly *"deep"* ones.

Here is the most simple, most important, and deepest truth Paul prayed for the early believers to understand-

> *"...so that Christ may **dwell in** your hearts through faith; and that you, being **rooted and grounded in love**, may be able to **comprehend** with all the saints what is the breadth and length and height and depth, and to know the **love of Christ** which **surpasses knowledge**, that you may be filled up to all the fullness of God."*
>
> (Eph. 3:17-19)

Filled up to the fullness of God...by knowing the depth of His love for you?! **It just doesn't get any deeper than this!**

Fellowship Through Meditation

Meditation is a very important part of our fellowship with God. Don't be afraid of it. Meditation was God's idea long before New Agers thought of it and Eastern religions perverted it. What makes the activity of meditation healthy or unhealthy comes from what we meditate upon.

When we meditate on His word and behold His beauty through worship, then meditation becomes an important means of fellowship and we are enabled to put our faith in the true things. And this kind of faith makes it all real.

When Joshua was preparing to lead God's people into the Promised Land, he was told the key to his success would be learning to fellowship God by meditating on His word day and night.

> *"This book of the law shall not depart from your mouth, but you shall **meditate** on it day and night."*
>
> (Joshua 1:8)

The biblical word for **meditate** means *"to ponder on it, to repeat it, to roll it over and over in your mind"*. The Holy Spirit, the true Teacher, speaks to us as we see the simple meaning of God's word and meditate upon it. Our thinking is renewed as we take the simple truth of God's word and ponder it; roll it over and over in our minds.

David understood the power of true meditation and spoke of its power in the Psalms; even under the Old Covenant.

> *"Make me understand the way of Your precepts, so I will **meditate** on Your wonders."*
>
> (Ps. 119:27)

> "*My eyes anticipate the night watches, that I may **meditate** on Your word.*"
>
> (Ps. 119:148)

> "*I will remember my song in the night; I will **meditate** with my heart and my spirit **ponders**…*"
>
> (Ps. 77:6)

> "*One thing I have asked from the LORD, that I shall seek: that I may dwell in the house of the LORD all the days of my life, to behold the beauty of the LORD and to **meditate** in His temple.*"
>
> (Ps. 27:4)

Meditation In The New Covenant

Paul tells us the same thing is true for us as we seek to live in the freedom of the New Covenant. His instruction was to feed and focus on what is true, honorable, pure, lovely, of good report, excellent and worthy of praise.

> "*Finally, brethren, whatever is true, whatever is honorable, whatever is right, whatever is pure, whatever is lovely, whatever is of good repute, if there is any excellence and if anything worthy of praise, dwell on these things.*"
>
> (Phil. 4:8)

Of course, all these qualities are found in Christ and in the truth of what He has already done for us. Seeing what He has already done for us draws us into interacting through worship.

Focus On Him By Framing Our Worship on New Covenant Truth

We have been learning the truth of *What He is really like* and *How He really feels about us*. These simple, eternal truths should cause true, spiritual worship to explode within us!

Much of the current teaching on worship seems to have gotten very complicated. But to Paul and the early believers, worship was the simple, natural result of seeing *What He is really like* and *How He really feels about us*; and then letting the Spirit worship in and through us.

Paul makes it clear that worship is about learning to simply cry out as sons to our Father and put our entire focus on Him. The focus of our worship must not be on our adversary, our battles or our lack of perfectly understanding His will for us.

But our focus must be on Him; His awesome beauty, His supreme majesty, His unequaled power, His perfect holiness, His everlasting goodness; and His unending love for us! This must be framed by the truth that we are not orphans, we are His children.

True worship is supposed to be the simplicity of children crying out in love to their Father. The early believers had none of the various helps and aids we have today, but they did

Children Crying Out To Our Father

> *"For you have not received a spirit of slavery leading to fear again, but you have received a spirit of adoption as sons by which we cry out, '**Abba! Father!**' The Spirit Himself testifies with our spirit that we are children of God..."*
>
> (Rom. 8:15-16)

Abba! Father! This is a phrase that does not translate very well in English because it seems like just repetition. But it is a term of deep affection and it is based on the relationship of confident son-ship. Most literally, it means, ***"Father, my dear Father!"***, and it pours out of the heart of sons.

Worship should never be any more complicated than this: children crying out to our Father with deep love and affection. As we feed on the truth that He has already fully accepted us as His children, worship should naturally come pouring out of us, regardless of our immediate circumstances.

And to insure that worship does come pouring out of us, He causes His Spirit to worship in and through us.

The Spirit Worships Within Us

> *"Because you are sons, God has sent forth the Spirit of His Son into our hearts, crying, "**Abba! Father!**"*
>
> (Gal. 4:6)

Worship pours out of us when we see the truth of our sonship to the Father. The Spirit of His Son enables us to worship this simple way because He is already crying out within us. We must learn to get in tune with the Spirit in us. He is already in us, worshipping through us. Get in tune with Him!

And it's not complicated. Just let the Spirit help you find as many ways as you can to say, *"**Father, my dear Father!**"* Let the Spirit worship *in* you and *through* you.

Faith Is The Natural Result

As we feed ourselves on the truths of His word concerning the New Covenant, and we frame our worship with the truths of this New Covenant, faith is the natural result. Faith is not the result of my labor, effort or hard work. It's the natural result of constantly feeding on Him!

Faith is listed as both a fruit and a gift of the Spirit. (Gal. 5:22, 1 Cor.12) Jesus is the author and finisher of our faith. (Heb. 12:2) Faith is not something we must work up or talk ourselves into. Faith is the natural result of feeding on His word, and focusing our hearts and minds upon Him in worship.

A child's faith in their parents care for them is simply based on growing up in the love of the parent. Our faith is simply based on growing up in our knowledge of His love and care for us.

Simple Faith Brings Transformation

As we learn to *feed* on what the Word actually tells us about *what God is really like* and *how He really feels about us*, we can worship Him in spirit and truth. As we *focus* on His truthfulness, His faithfulness and the beauty of His majesty through worship, our simple, growing *faith* causes mysterious and miraculous transformation to happen; *to* us, *in* us and *through* us.

> *"But we all, with unveiled face, beholding as in a mirror the glory of the Lord, are **being transformed** into the same image from glory to glory, just as from the Lord, the Spirit."*
>
> (2 Cor 3:18)

This miraculous, progressive transformation is what the New Covenant is all about. This is ***God's Brilliant Plan*** of Christ living His live *in* and *through* us.

And this, my fellow seeker, is what real life is all about!

Another great resource for your journey from *Mark Drake*

I believe that for the early disciples, the New Covenant was not so much about "*just believe in Jesus*", but much more about "*believe Jesus is living in you*". I believe this is what actually made the New Covenant…NEW!

For a far more in-depth examination of this great mystery of Christ living in and through us, you may want to read my book, **God's Brilliant Plan** – *Searching for the Easy and Light Life Jesus Promised.*

This book, CDs, DVDs, and other similar resources about the nature of true grace and New Covenant life, are available at markdrake.org.

We would love to hear from you about your own journey into the true grace of God and how our resources have impacted your thinking. Please write us about your story.

Just a few of the many resources available:

God's Brilliant Plan – book – 250 pages – soft cover

God's Brilliant Plan – Study Guide – goes through book page by page

God's Brilliant Plan – Audio Book – read by author on 8 CDs

God's Brilliant Plan – Live Seminar on DVD – 8 sessions / 10 hours

God's Brilliant Plan – Live Audio Seminar on CD – 8 sessions / 10 hours

Build an Unshakable Life – 4 audio CDs

Changing From the Inside Out – 4 audio CDs

Grace – The Unearned Power to Change – 1 & 2 – 8 CD set

How God Feels about Me – 4 audio CDs

How to live without Disappointment – 4 audio CDs

Power of Christ's Life In and Through Us – 4 audio CDs

Sanctifying Power of the Spirit – 4 audio CDs

Why God Must Run Us Out of Our Strength – 4 audio CDs

Offense, Forgiveness and Freedom – 4 audio CDs

...and many more!

Visit us at markdrake.org

Would you consider joining us as a monthly partner?

We can share in the fruit together as you help send us to train leaders and provide free resources in some of the world's poorest places...where the Kingdom of God is exploding!

From the jungles, to the barrios, to the slums, to the world's major cities; we are training leaders to train others with the message of true Grace and how to live in the New Covenant.

What We Do For You As A Monthly Partner

We want you to keep growing in grace, so we will send you free teaching CDs several times a year and offer you large discounts on all our new books, DVDs and CDs.

As a monthly partner, you will receive a newsletter each month telling you where we are and what we are accomplishing together. You will also receive email prayer updates. We pledge to pray for you as you pray for us! Just go to markdrakeministries.com to check out partnership.

How We Handle Our Partners' Money

We are deeply indebted to all who sow their hard-earned money into our lives and ministry. Your generosity and belief in our mission, message and methods are what enable us to accomplish all we do in some of the world's poorest places.

We have chosen to live a modest lifestyle. We do not believe we have to "*prove our faith*" by living extravagantly nor do we believe God's people must be poor in order to be holy. We just believe we must be faithful stewards with the money people freely contribute to us.

Our office is in our home. We are a family ministry with a few volunteers. We pay all our own travel expenses. We travel at the lowest cost available. We keep our costs down so we can minister in places many others can't or don't go. We have frontline missionaries and leaders around the world who count on us for support and resources.

We don't hire fund-raising companies or purchase donor lists for solicitation. We do not use manipulation to prey on the compassion of good people. We don't make unscriptural promises of quick riches if you give to our ministry. We try to honestly share the needs and opportunities, and trust you to do what's right for you. We know that God will provide for you and for us.

We know you sacrifice to give to our ministry and we want you to know your money is being used honorably. MDM, Inc. is designated by the IRS as a 501(c)3 non-profit, tax exempt organization and is accountable to a non-paid board of directors and our church family in St Louis, MO.